THREE
STRIPES
SOUTH

THREE
STRIPES
SOUTH

The 1,000km trek that
inspired a women's
adventure movement

BEX BAND

Bradt GUIDES

First published in the UK in August 2021 by
Bradt Guides Ltd
31a High Street, Chesham, HP5 1BW, England
www.bradtguides.com

Print edition published in the USA by The Globe Pequot Press Inc,
PO Box 480, Guilford, Connecticut 06437-0480

Text copyright © 2021 Bex Band
Edited by Samantha Cook
Maps copyright © 2021 Bradt Guides Ltd; includes map data © OpenStreetMap contributors

Cover design by Ollie Davis Illustration; www.olliedavisillustration.com
Layout and typesetting by Ian Spick, Bradt Guides & www.dataworks.co.in
Map by David McCutcheon FBCart.S
Production managed by Sue Cooper, Bradt Guides & Zenith Media

ISBN: 9781784778385

British Library Cataloguing in Publication Data
A catalogue record for this book is available from the British Library

Digital conversion by www.dataworks.co.in

Printed in the UK by Zenith Media

About the author

Bex Band inspires others to go on outdoor adventures through writing, speaking and leading expeditions. Her passion for adventure began when, despite being both unfit and inexperienced, she decided to hike the length of Israel, a distance of more than 1,000 kilometres.

Noticing a gender imbalance in outdoor sports, Bex launched Love Her Wild, a women's adventure community. Providing support and opportunities, the community has taken thousands of women on adventures around the world.

Bex has been recognised by *Business Leader* as one of the UK's top thirty inspirational entrepreneurs and was awarded a Next Generation Award by Enterprise Nation. She has been shortlisted for a National Diversity Award for her work advocating for women in adventure and was given 'Legacy Maker' status on San Miguel's alternative 'Rich List'.

Acknowledgements

Juggling a newborn, a global pandemic and a book deal was only made possible thanks to my wonderful adventure and life partner, Gil. I am forever grateful for your support and determination to co-parent so that neither of us should have to sacrifice our dreams.

I wondered if I was taking on too much as a new parent, but I have been blessed with the most relaxed daughter – you never complained as I typed one-handed while nursing you or balanced a laptop on my knees while you slept on me. Thank you Rivi for bringing so much joy and inspiration into my life. I'm very proud to be your mum!

Thank you to my own mum (Barbara Band) for filling my life with books and words. To my author friends, Emma Rosen and Emily Hunt, for helping me through the publishing process. To my writing group – Iona, Thys, Soraya, Emma, Alison, Ruth and Catherine – for keeping me accountable through lockdowns. To Jennifer Barclay and the team at Bradt for making this book a reality. And last, but not least, my blog readers, followers and all the amazing women in the Love Her Wild community: thank you for the ongoing support. I never take it for granted.

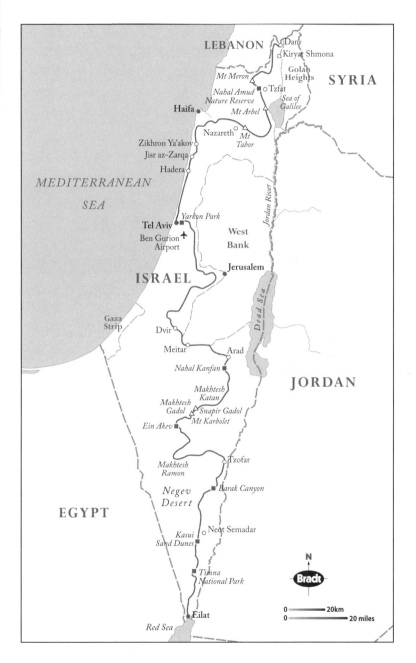

Chapter 1

Is there anything more reliable in life than a toilet cubicle? Locked in a familiar cocoon of white walls, knowing this space is, temporarily, only for you, you are offered a few moments of uninterrupted peace to do as you please. You can simply sit there looking dishevelled without needing to care, give yourself the headspace to conjure up an internal pep talk or waste time on your phone away from judgemental stares.

It was in a toilet cubicle that I found myself trying to calm my nerves after a noisy flight and the chaotic mayhem that is Israeli airport arrivals. I'd had to answer a dozen questions on who I was and where I'd come from to get through. When I eventually received the stamp of approval, saying that I was granted entry, my stress levels increased even more. The reason for my being in the country suddenly felt very real and I had the overwhelming feeling I was spinning downhill out of control, past the point of being able to slam on the brakes.

Usually, arriving in a foreign airport is accompanied by excitement as you anticipate all the joyous fun that lies ahead on your holiday. This was different, though. I'd gone to Israel not to spend time on a beach or to explore the many sites of the Holy Land, but to take on the biggest, most daunting challenge of my life – and I was seriously starting to question if I'd made a terrible mistake.

A flight announcement on the overhead speakers brought me back to reality and the white walls of the cubicle. I left the safety of the toilets to rejoin Gil who was waiting outside with our luggage, checking his phone for the umpteenth time since landing. My husband was anxious for an altogether different reason. His parents had made the three-hour round trip from their home town to come meet us off the plane at Tel Aviv and it wasn't fair for me to keep him from them any longer.

I heard the squeal of excitement from my mother-in-law as we turned the final corner of the airport maze, hitting a wall of waiting loved ones and taxi drivers. Mira and Amir stood among them, their smiles beaming. There were hugs, more squealing and then more hugs. Amir, my father-in-law, took my face in his large hands, forcing me to look at him, then gently slapped my cheek twice in a gesture that made me think of *The Godfather*. I'd like to say that this effusive welcome was because it had been so long since we'd last seen them, but Israeli greetings, especially in Gil's family, were drawn-out and affectionate even if you were just returning from an hour's trip to the supermarket.

Amir bent down, picked up my large rucksack and threw it over his broad shoulder with ease, before making his way towards the exit.

'You are really doing this hike, then?' he said in his gruff voice, thick with accent. It was exactly the question I'd been asking myself on repeat throughout the entire flight. Was I really going to do this hike?

Of course, the border control officer, with her mass of curly hair unsuccessfully tied back in a bun, had wanted to know why I was visiting Israel. I'd thought about making up a lie, thinking my real reason might seem too far-fetched, but concluded that this was definitely not the place to be trying to distort the truth. Israeli border control was ruthless and unforgiving.

'I'm walking the Israel National Trail,' I'd told her with forced conviction.

She looked up from my passport, one eyebrow raised. 'The whole thing?'

'Yes.'

'Really?'

'Yes,' I insisted, shifting from one leg to the other. While I'd been making my plans and talking to people about walking the 1,020-kilometre Israel National Trail for months now, I realised that this border control officer was one of the few people I'd said it out loud to who had actually heard of the trail, and who knew the scale of the challenge that Gil and I had signed up for.

'How long will it take?'

'About eight weeks in total.'

She looked back at my passport, at her computer screen, then held my gaze, looking at me for more than was comfortable. I stood still and tried hard to ignore my instinct to glance away or smile, worried that my nerves would make it seem as though I was lying. After what felt like a really long time, she leant over and grabbed a stamp, slamming it down hard.

'Good luck,' she said, my passport slung casually between her fingers as she handed it back, already looking past me at the next person in line. 'You'll need it. It's hot.'

Hot it was. Stepping out of the cool, air-conditioned airport, we walked into a wall of heat. I took a deep breath. The dusty air and heavy humidity was suffocating, making my lungs feel like they needed to work that extra bit harder just to get enough oxygen in. Amir's hand, which was still softly holding the back of my neck and guiding me forward, gave a squeeze. He was waiting for an answer.

'Yep. I guess so, Amir. We're really doing this hike.'

* * * *

I'd first heard of the Israel National Trail while sitting at my desk, scrolling through social media, having just taken a bite of my Marmite sandwich. I was coming to the end of a year of teacher training and, just like in all my previous jobs, break times were my favourite part of the day. I often used them to escape in the maze of the internet, daydreaming, being nosy and making plans for my weekends and time off.

The usual content whizzed past me on the screen, updates from friends, adverts and interesting articles shared, when a word caught my eye, *Adventure*. It was part of a heading that led me to an article about the best hikes in the world, and that's where I saw it for the first time: the Israel National Trail.

I immediately left the article to do a search so I could find out more, landing on the official page for the trail. The Israel National Trail is a hike stretching the full length of the country, from the Israel-Lebanon border to Eilat on the Gulf of Aqaba. It passes mountains in the north, follows the coastline to Tel Aviv and heads through thick forests near Jerusalem before cutting straight across the Negev, a huge desert which covers more than half of the country.

There were other hikes featured in the article but this one immediately stood out because of my ties to the country. Israel had never been on my radar, but then neither had meeting a future husband, certainly not one from a different country. I had been by Lake Atitlán in Guatemala travelling and learning Spanish, shortly after finishing university. It just so happened that the week I joined the Spanish school there was only one other beginner starting at the same time. I met Gil in the afternoon Conversation Club after our one-to-one lessons had finished. Fresh from his mandatory army service, tanned, with dark features, he oozed endless optimism and was enjoying life in the way that only a 22-year-old can. It didn't take me long to fall completely in love. In fact, it was just a week later that I found myself in an internet café on a phone call with my mum declaring I had met the man I wanted to marry.

'A Guatemalan?!' she said excitedly.

'Uh, no. Actually he's Israeli.'

'OK. Well, make sure you're being safe.' My mum took my hopeful declaration of marriage in her stride, as I knew she would. She told me to just enjoy myself, although I picked up on a hint of scepticism about the situation. I felt it too. A girl from Basingstoke and a boy from Israel meeting in a Spanish school in Guatemala, although romantic, would surely never work out.

Just four months later, though, and Gil was on a plane to the UK to start a new life with me in London, a city that was new for both of us. Despite there being a fresh coating of snow on the ground outside, he walked out of the terminal wearing nothing more than shorts, sandals and a knitted jumper he'd picked up in a market in Central America. First stop was a shopping mall, where I bought him a late Hanukkah present: a coat and a pair of woolly socks.

The very existence of long-distance trails was a completely new discovery for me. It amazed me that there were people out there that did these sorts of things, real-life adventurers. I was finding out that our country had things like national parks and mountain ranges, environments that were alien to me. I began devouring books, magazines, films and talks by adventurers, fascinated by it all. Time and again I heard the same message: 'If I can do this, you can too; anything is possible if you put your mind to it'. I heard this from people who had climbed Everest, or rowed an ocean or cycled around the world. Hugely expensive, physically demanding feats that were so far removed from what I knew. Almost all the adventurers I saw fitted one type of mould. White men who oozed the distinct and unshakable confidence instilled by a public-school upbringing. They wore bushy beards and displayed cabinets filled with evidence of sporting achievements and awards they'd collected in their younger years. They had a need to conquer, claiming world firsts and record-breaking feats. I was far from fitting in to the world of adventure. Unfit and inexperienced in the outdoors, I hated regular exercise, trauma from my overweight days and humiliating PE classes never quite having left me. I'd collected far more detentions in my school years than awards. I wasn't a hiker or a camper and didn't know how to navigate using a map and, worse still, I didn't even have any outdoorsy friends or family that I could ask for advice.

The Israel National Trail would be a huge undertaking, something that felt scary and beyond me, but still, I was drawn to it and, even more, to the emotions it stirred up inside me when I imagined standing on the trail, a large bag on my back and a dramatic landscape up ahead. The truth was I was feeling like a failure at life, like nothing I started came to completion, like, no matter how hard I tried, I couldn't quite find solid ground. While friends around me began climbing their way up successful careers and putting down deposits on shiny new builds, I was struggling to find the motivation to even get out of bed most days. I knew I needed a change and perhaps this hike would be it. A challenge and a chance to prove myself.

The decision to do the hike, taken just like that, still chewing on the last bites of my Marmite sandwich, would send me sprinting down a new path in life. It was a fleeting moment, a chance discovery and a brave decision, but first there was a tiny obstacle: I would need to let my husband know that he would be joining me. If this was going to happen, if I was really going to dismantle our lives to take on this obscure challenge, we'd need to be in it together.

* * * *

I watched Gil take off his suit and slip into more comfortable clothes. The lounge and bedroom shared the same space in our split-level Putney studio. I saw his demeanour change as it did every night, the stresses and strains of his busy City job stripping away as the tie came off, slung over a clothes hanger, ready for the next morning. He joined me on the sofa and looked at me expectantly, sensing I had something to say. I shifted in my seat.

'You know I'm not very happy at the moment?'

Gil nodded, gently taking my hand in his.

'I need a change. I think we both need a change, actually.'

When we first moved to London, five years earlier, we made a list of a hundred things we wanted to do in the city. It was a time of playful fun, imagining all the places we would visit. On weekends we'd head out into the centre to see museums, take boat tours along the Thames, watch shows or take selfies in front of landmarks. There had been some more out-there ideas thrown in the mix as well. One day we'd thrown away our inhibitions to join a flash mob and on another occasion we managed to blag our way behind the scenes of a Rolling Stones concert in Hyde Park. With just twenty things left to go, though, the list had been left tacked on our wardrobe untouched for almost two years. Something had shifted. Absorbed as we were in work, chasing promised promotions and an ever-growing pile of paperwork, free time now felt like a luxury reserved only for catching up with sleep, food shopping and laundry, not for having fun.

'I think we should both leave our jobs and hike the Israel National Trail.'

Gil's eyebrows shot up. Although his family had exposed him to things like day hiking and camping, you were more likely to find him in his youth in the lighting box in a drama hall than on the sports field. He, like me, had slotted in well to the unfit convenience lifestyle of city living and was not someone you would expect to see doing a long-distance hike.

He was now fiddling with the wedding ring on his finger; eight months on, he still couldn't get used to wearing it.

'When do you want to go?'

'I was thinking towards the end of this year. They say it takes about two months to do the whole thing. I can only get a three-month visa to visit the country, so it wouldn't give us a lot of time if we needed a few days beforehand to prepare, but we should be able to manage it.' There are only two safe windows for hiking the Israel National Trail, one in spring and one in autumn. The desert is a dangerous place to be in summer, when the temperatures soar, and in winter, when the risk of flash flooding is at its highest. Although it was only February, I knew spring would be too soon to get everything ready and to have saved up the money we would need to complete the hike, which made autumn our next window of opportunity.

'But I'd miss my end-of-year bonus.'

Not just the bonus, I thought, knowing there would be a lot more sacrifices made. 'You would. But we've been saying for ages that we want to go away. There's always going to be a reason not to do it. I just feel like… it just feels like we should…' I tailed off, not sure how to explain how it just felt right in my gut, even if every rational thought was telling me it was wrong, that doing the hike didn't make any sense at all.

'And our jobs?'

'I'll have finished my teacher training by then, so could probably just pick up a teaching job when I get back. And maybe you could ask for a sabbatical.' We both knew Gil's job would never approve one. Agreeing to this hike would mean saying goodbye to the job he had worked so hard to get, along with the promotion that his manager had been hinting at. We would be losing our financial security and savings. I also wasn't sure how easy it would be to get a teaching job after taking a break straight after completing my training. There would be a lot of uncertainty hanging over our return.

He sighed and looked out of the window at the Tube crossing Putney Bridge, the train windows steamed up from the squashed commuters inside who were lit up against the drab, dark winter sky. 'Don't the trains passing by bother you?' guests would always ask when they felt the flat shake like a mild earthquake every few minutes. They never did. I didn't even notice the shaking anymore.

Gil turned back to me. 'The Israel National Trail,' he said, as if playing with the words out loud, before a slight grin appeared in the corner of his mouth. 'I'm in. Let's do it.'

The next day we booked our flights. It felt like the signature at the end of a contract, the seal of an envelope. We had cemented our decision.

Could it really be that easy? The hike felt like such a momentous thing, but the hardest part of getting to the start had been the simple act of just saying yes.

What followed was a methodical taking apart of our lives, chipping away at a to-do list one task after another. With the click of an email, we left the careers we had spent years working towards. We decluttered and reduced our possessions and handed in the notice on our flat. We moved in with family for our final weeks and had our goodbye parties with friends. All my spare time was now reserved for searching the internet desperately looking for answers to all the things I didn't know: 'How hard is it to hike one thousand kilometres?' 'How do you go to the toilet outdoors?' 'What animals can kill you in the desert?'

Finally, all that was left was our boarding passes and two bulky backpacks that sat in the corner of our temporary bedroom. Looking at all the shiny and perfectly organised gear, I couldn't decide if it made me feel more prepared and ready for the trail or more like I was well and truly out of my depth. Either way, and despite all the nerves and doubting, the presence of the packs made me certain of one thing. It felt good to be doing something different, taking a proactive step, shaking up our lives.

Maybe this would turn out to be a good decision or maybe it wouldn't. One thing was certain, though. This was going to be an adventure.

Chapter 2

I unclipped the straps on my bag and let it fall before swiftly following. My weak muscles gave up halfway and I fell back, colliding with the ground with a thud. Pulling at the laces on my boots, I yanked them off, along with my damp socks, freeing my swollen and bruised feet, before laying back down, using my rucksack as a pillow. I let my arms fall to the side so I was in the shape of a giant starfish.

The coarse grass under me was sharp against my bare skin but I barely registered it; all I could focus on was the overwhelming heat radiating from my body, desperate to escape. The shade from the nearby eucalyptus tree offered some relief, although I longed for even just a slight breeze to move the painfully still, humid air around me. It didn't matter, though: it only mattered that I didn't have to move, that, at least for a short amount of time, I didn't have to hike.

'This is absolute bliss,' I said to Gil who had ended up in the same starfish position next to me, also with his boots off.

'Uh-huh,' he managed, before a moment later adding, 'I'm ravenous.'

His declaration made me immediately aware of my own hunger pangs. I sat up faster than I had intended and began pulling food from the top of my backpack. We had just gone to the corner shop across the park and had bought way too much food, despite knowing it wouldn't last long in this mid-afternoon heat. I just couldn't resist the rows of chilled fresh fruit and treats that lined the shelves. As I greedily threw items in the basket I caught the lady at the checkout staring at me and felt self-conscious imagining the sweaty, red-faced mess that she must be looking at. When I'd gone to pay, like a dog longing for praise I'd told her we were walking the trail and had just come from Dan, but she'd simply offered a robotic smile in response.

'An easy start' had been promised online, but that was not what it had been. Just a day and a half into the hike and I felt alarmed at the thought of hiking any further. This was far from easy. This was tough, too tough, and I had barely even started.

* * * *

Leaving Gil's parents' house before dawn the day before, it had taken us two buses and three hours to reach the start of the trail, a place called Dan, which sits in the corner of Israel near the border of Lebanon, Syria and the Golan Heights. I spent much of the journey staring out of the window trying to ignore the barrel of the M15 rifle that kept jabbing my ribs each time we turned a corner. The bus was full of young soldiers returning to work after observing Yom Kippur with their families and I'd been squished up next to one of them, a boy still in his teens who, after checking his social media on his phone, had opted for sleep, slumped over his weapon carelessly. I studied the M15 to see if it was loaded and if the safety catch was on, but had no idea what I was looking for. ·

Young soldiers wearing the standard loose dark green uniform are a common sight in Israel. I tried to remember being his age and what it would have felt like if my university years had instead been replaced with mandatory army service and lugging a heavy weapon with me everywhere I went, but it was hard to fathom.

'This is our stop,' Gil called back from the seat in front, causing my insides to twist in a knot. When the bus pulled over I squeezed myself around the young soldier, who was reluctant to stand up, and began the obstacle course of stepping over the other soldiers who were sat in the walkway engrossed in their phones or sleeping. It was not an easy task in my large walking boots, which made my feet extra bulky. Because our feet swell up when hiking, I'd been told to buy a size up from my usual in order to help prevent blisters and my nails from falling off. Both these scenarios sounded painful so I'd gladly followed the advice, even if it did make me even more clumsy when I walked.

The door closed behind us and the bus drove off, leaving a cloud of dust behind it and then nothing but silence. The task of hiking the trail loomed in front of me like an overbearing physical presence. We had been dropped by the side of a deserted road opposite a wonky handwritten sign that said 'INT', short for Israel National Trail, with an arrow pointing down a side path. I could already feel sweat dripping down the back of my neck and I hadn't even started moving.

'Let's get going,' Gil muttered, more to himself than to me. 'I'll help you with your bag.' He had been unusually quiet during the journey, spending much of the time chewing at his nails, a bad habit that came and went. He'd been so wrapped up in the excitement of seeing his family I think he'd forgotten our reason for coming to Israel. There was no hiding away from that fact any longer, though.

Gil picked up my rucksack and took its thirteen-kilo weight while I put my arms through and did up the straps, a thick one around the waist and a second, smaller one across the chest. The hip strap had a small pocket where I'd stored, in preparation, a couple of snack bars ready for pit stops during the day. While Gil busied himself with getting his own bag on, I tightened the straps and then tested the weight by taking a few steps, the first time I'd tried my bag done up fully and while wearing all my hiking gear. The bag made me feel sluggish and the weight sat heavy on my shoulders, pulling them backwards and causing me to lean forward slightly to keep my balance. I tried readjusting the straps, looking for a combination that made it lighter or pull less on the shoulders but nothing seemed to help.

There was no point delaying the inevitable any longer. Without another word, and with hiking poles in hand, I crossed the road and began down the path, Gil following quietly behind me.

At the end of the path we reached the official start of the trail, another underwhelming sign, and spotted our first marker. The entire trail is signposted with waymarkers painted on to rocks, walls and posts; these would save us from having to rely too heavily on maps for navigation. Each marker shows three stripes: one white, one blue and one orange. The stripes signify the three stages of the trail: the mountains of the north, which sometimes see snow in winter; the blue coastline of the centre; and then, finally, the huge orange desert in the south. The stripes are never aligned, but instead are staggered like steps to let hikers know which direction they are going in and to ensure that they don't accidentally start following the trail the wrong way. As we were heading from north to south, we'd be following the markers that showed the orange stripe at the highest point, the top step, indicating that we were heading in the direction of the desert.

We both stood looking at the sign as if waiting for a band to appear to give us a fanfare and mark what felt like a momentous moment.

'Let's take a picture,' I said, feeling that this was what hikers who walk long-distance trails did. Using my hard-wearing compact camera, which promised to be dust-, water- and drop-proof, I took an awkward selfie of us with the sign in the background. 'Now we can compare this to a picture of us at the end of the trail.'

Gil nodded. A bird chirped somewhere in the distance.

Without another moment's thought, I walked past the marker and on to the path. I was officially on the trail. After months of planning and prepping it was finally happening.

The reality of hiking was nothing like I had my imagined. Most of my daydreaming had occurred on my commutes, taking the overground to and from work in London, and I realised now they had been far too glamorous. For starters, I'd never given enough thought to the copious amounts of sweating I would be doing. It was nearing midday by the time we started on the trail so the sun was directly above us, beating down on our heads with all its sickening thirty degrees and without a wisp of cloud in sight. To protect me from the glare I wore a sun hat and a thin long-sleeved shirt over my vest and shorts. Although it kept me shaded, underneath the layers I felt like I was suffocating, cooking in an oven. My clothes were soaking within minutes.

I also hadn't given much thought to the dust. I coughed, my throat feeling dry, and, when lifting my hand to wipe sweat from my forehead, found I was already covered in a layer of dirt. Worst of all, though, was the effort of physically moving under the weight of the bag, which was already starting to rub and dig in painful places. My legs felt like lead and every muscle in my cumbersome body screamed at me to stop walking.

I'd barely made it an hour before I started to imagine how I might escape this, how we could turn back and wait for the next bus back to Gil's home town. Perhaps I could fake an injury to explain our reason for quitting so quickly. *This is just the beginning*, I kept saying to myself on repeat, knowing I could very easily drown in my own self-doubt; *it will get easier.* I wasn't convinced it would but, for now, the deception seemed like a good illusion to cling on to.

The path meandered through rows of harvested crops, barren hills off in the distance, although I barely looked up or took stock of my surroundings. Heavy with a backpack full of supplies, heavy with emotion and heavy with the heat, I settled into nothing more than the few steps ahead. That alone took all my concentration. There was no plan, no tomorrow, only the manageable existence of the hundred metres or so of path that lay immediately in front of me.

My heart swelled with relief a few hours in when I saw the small stone wall at the next turning. It was the perfect size to sit on while taking the weight of the bag without needing to take it off. If I took it off I might never have the energy to get it back on again.

'Fancy stopping for lunch?' I asked Gil, the first thing I'd said to him since starting.

'Sure,' he said, mouth open, panting for air. Before joining me on the wall, he took our lunch from the top of my bag and handed it to me. I carefully unwrapped the kitchen paper to reveal two large slices of mushroom Wellington, leftovers from Yom Kippur, a dish his Auntie Yael had made for us especially. Had that really only been yesterday?

We had landed in Israel in early October, just in time for the Jewish observance, which meant that the day before starting the hike had consisted of a big family gathering organised by Amir and Mira. I was earning serious brownie points with my in-laws for doing this hike and the news of our arrival had spread through the large Drori family and beyond like wildfire. The grandparents, aunties, uncles and cousins came together to see us, and the day was filled with eating, drinking and randomly bursting into song. After the meal, the stories got louder and more exaggerated with each sip, often resulting in sibling squabbles or heated debates. While the kids ran around in circles and the adults continued to fill their wine glasses, I snuck upstairs. We were staying in the room where Gil grew up, and remnants of his past still dotted the shelves: a schoolbook, his army beret and stickers of album covers from his favourite bands. I curled up on the bed, hugging a pillow close to me, and thought of home. Of our friends in London who were probably out now having drinks, tucked up on the sofa watching TV or maybe cooking dinner and talking about their days. It all felt so far away and I wished so much that I could be there too, in the comfort of our flat in London. If I could snap my fingers, undo this decision and not have to go ahead with the hike, I would do it in an instant. But this was not an option. We'd gone too far for that. Made too many changes, told too many people, and now here we were in Israel with a big gathering full of well-intentioned questions and attention that just seemed to be making the pressure even worse.

'You doing alright?' I asked Gil as I took another mouthful of the delicious Wellington along with a large swig of water.

'Yes,' he said, a little strained. 'You?'

'I'm fine.' We were clearly both mutual in our thinking that there was nothing to be gained from saying out loud how hard we were both finding this.

* * * *

I opened our trail guidebook and flicked through the pages. The first thing we had done when preparing for the trip was order a book online called *Hike the Land of Israel*. It contained all the maps we needed for each stage of the trail, along with useful tips on where to find water and camping spots along the way. Some people online referred to it simply as the 'Red Book' and it was just that. A red book with a few pictures of the trail on the front and page upon page of descriptive writing about mileage, accents and water stations. Although the trail was well marked, I don't know how anyone could have managed without the information the book contained on water resources and, although we could have worked out our accommodation as we went, the Red Book made it a lot easier, marking out clearly what was allowed and where we might find hidden spots.

Finding the dog-eared page that marked the map for today's section of the trail, I calculated how far we'd come, eager to know distance covered and distance left to go. I then checked it again, as if I could somehow magically draw an extra kilometre to this point, but the same figure came up. Despite all the effort and discomfort we'd only walked a total of seven kilometres. I put the map away and instead settled on watching a bird of prey circling above our heads until Gil said it was probably time we carried on.

One marker at a time, one step at a time.

We passed a nature reserve which we opted to walk around rather than cut through to save having to pay the entrance fee, wary that we had limited funds for the trip, then found ourselves on a particularly tedious long stretch of road where we were disturbed by only a few passing cars.

Dusk was approaching when we entered woodland, making our way up a steep path until it levelled out near the top. It was there that we spotted a perfectly flat section, the exact size needed to set up our tent. We both agreed we should stop. Although we had seen some potential camping options a little earlier, I was eager to reach the woods, hopeful they would provide a bit of security and shelter given that we would be camping out alone in the wild. It was a pretty spot. We were nestled among the pine trees and a couple of hundred metres below us we could make out the outskirts of the small city of Kiryat Shmona. When dark set in, lights from the city were visible through the trees, twinkling as the branches swayed in the wind.

Despite being hidden by the trees, I felt uncomfortably exposed at the thought of sleeping in this random place for the night. It didn't feel right to sleep somewhere that wasn't a bed or a spot marked with a sign saying 'campsite'. I kept looking up and down the path as if waiting for someone to come and tell us we weren't allowed to be here, or, worse, to rob us of our possessions. At least the tiredness from the day made my head so foggy it helped take the edge off a bit. We had walked a total of fourteen kilometres to this point and I concluded it had been one of the toughest days of my life both physically and emotionally. All the thinking, the pressure, the doubting, along with the walking and carrying, had been too much. I was exhausted and had little energy left to carry out the tasks involved in ensuring I had a bed and something to eat that night.

'I don't think I could have gone any further,' Gil said as he pulled the tent out of his bag, undoing the cord and laying out its contents on the floor.

'Me either,' I admitted, trying not to think about the fact that, because my visa allowed me only ninety days in the country, most days on the trail would involve, on average, hiking twenty-five kilometres. Right now, that seemed impossible to maintain.

Once we'd put up the tent, Gil suggested he inflate the roll mats while I start dinner, clearly feeling the same hunger pangs that I did. I rummaged in my bag for the sack that contained all our supplies. Our food options on the trail were limited as we needed meals that were light and high in energy and, most importantly, could withstand the relentless heat. Sorting our supplies in the supermarket had taken a lot of time as we struggled to come up with suitable meals. We'd ended up with a mix of granola, nuts and dried fruit for snacks and breakfasts, pasta and couscous for dinners and rye bread with peanut butter for lunches. The latter turned out to be a terrible combination. Rye bread and peanut butter are both dense; put them together and you get a thick, sticky paste that is impossible to swallow without a swig of water to accompany it as it reluctantly journeys down the throat.

I decided on spaghetti for dinner, pulling out some stock cubes we'd brought for flavour as there were no handy pre-made sauces we could use that didn't come in a glass jar. I filled up our lightweight pan with water then got out our camping stove. The Jetboil stove is a really easy device to use. It screws on to a gas canister which you then turn on and light with a…

'Crap,' I said, dropping my head in my hands. 'We forgot to pack a lighter!'

The only thing worse than having rye bread and peanut butter for lunch is having to have rye bread and peanut butter for dinner as well.

Our mistake forgetting to pack the lighter meant that we had to push on the next day past our intended end point so we could take a small detour to a village named Ramot Naftali, which sat just off the trail. Walking through the deserted streets was like being in a ghost town, so it was a relief to reach the small corner shop and find it open.

We hadn't been able to face any more rye bread or peanut butter, so by now our hunger had reached a whole new level. Lying in the shade in the park, we laid all the food we had bought in front of us and started to tear open the packets. Hummus, pitta bread, tomatoes, crisps and cold juice was pushed into my mouth at a ferocious speed. Were we really only on the second day of hiking? My stomach was complaining as if it had been deprived of calories for weeks.

'I never noticed how much tastier food is when it's cold,' I said to Gil as I scooped another chunk of pitta bread in the hummus.

'I can't eat another mouthful.' Gil laid back down on the grass. The intensity of my own eating was also starting to slow. 'I'm going to nap for a bit. We've still got a couple of hours of light and not much further to go,' he added, already drifting off.

I thought about sleeping for a bit too, as I was also feeling tired, but decided against it. I didn't want to miss a second of the momentary relief that sitting down was bringing me. How good it was not to be walking. Not to be carrying a heavy bag. I twisted around and pulled the Red Book out of the side pocket of my bag. I studied the map, as I had done at every opportunity. We'd covered thirty-four kilometres to this point. That left 986 kilometres to go. My insides tensed. How could I possibly cover this distance when thirty-four kilometres had been so difficult and taken so much effort?

My concentration was broken by a large brown dog who came bounding over to us, escaping its owner from the other side of the park. He sniffed the ground where the food had been and then went over to Gil's bag and cocked his leg.

'HEY!' I yelled, jumping up as the dog ran off back towards his owner. Gil, now wide awake, was sniffing his bag, which caused me to burst out laughing.

'You wouldn't be laughing if it was your bag,' he grumbled.

'I don't think he peed on it. I scared him off just in time,' I said, adding, 'promise' when I saw how miserable he looked.

'It's not that,' he said. 'I don't feel…' Gil jumped up mid-sentence and ran to the bushes, where in quick succession he cleared his stomach of the food we'd just gorged on. Returning, he sat back down, the colour drained from his face.

'Maybe you ate too much?'

'I don't think so. I feel ill,' he groaned, clutching his stomach.

I took out our small red first-aid kit and rummaged inside looking for a hydration sachet. I made up a drink, mixing the contents of the sachet with water.

'Drink this slowly. And try lying down and resting a bit longer.' I surveyed our surroundings, noting the distinct stillness in the air that seems to occur when a hot day comes to an end. The shop over the road had since closed and, apart from the shop assistant and lone dog walker who had now left, we hadn't seen anyone all day. Gil needed to sleep properly, which meant we had to find somewhere to camp for the night. I ached for the security of four walls and a place to sleep that came equipped with a pillow and a lockable door.

'How bad are you feeling?' I asked Gil once he'd finished his drink. 'If you aren't well I could call your parents to come collect us and take us home until you feel better? Or maybe I could walk to one of the nearby houses to try to find someone to sort out booking a taxi. It'd take a while for anyone to get to us, but at least we're by roads.'

'No, I'm OK. I can walk a bit more.'

'Are you sure?' I asked, studying the map for flat, secluded spaces. 'Can you do another four kilometres? It looks like there are some options there where we can wild camp. It'd only be about another hour of walking.'

I was relieved when Gil agreed. Although nothing pleased me more than the thought of Gil's parents rescuing us, and arriving in the middle of the night at their home to a shower and a bed to sleep in, a little voice told me that if we left the trail now we would never come back.

I took a litre of water from Gil's bag and added it to my own to reduce the weight he was carrying by one kilo. It wasn't much but I hoped it would help a little.

After such a long time resting, the muscles in my legs stung angrily as I walked away from our shady spot, my shoulders and hips even more tender from where the bag was rubbing. I kept my complaints silent, though, knowing that Gil would be feeling even worse than me.

Leaving behind the ghost town we crossed a road, heading towards a factory. Stumbling over mounds of rotting waste that had been dumped outside the factory gates, I was pleased when we passed the boundary to a wide valley and wilderness once again. Behind the fences on our right were pomegranate trees, the bright red fruits large and inviting. Whatever used to be in the field to the left was long dead and abandoned, leaving nothing but a large space of rubble and brambles, unfortunately too rocky for camping.

'You doing OK?' I asked Gil.

'Yeah,' he replied, although I saw by the paleness of his face and the slump in his posture that he didn't mean it. I tried to give him words of encouragement as we walked, to keep him moving. 'We're so nearly there.' 'As soon as we have the tent up you can rest properly.' 'You'll probably be loads better in the morning.' Internally, I had none of the positivity I was outwardly expressing, feeling as though at any moment my body might just give up on me and refuse to move any further. At the rate we were going, though, we wouldn't reach the treeline before dark. An hour had passed and we'd barely shuffled more than two kilometres.

Stepping to the side of the track, Gil dropped his bag and slumped against the fence.

'I can't go any further,' he said, removing his sun hat and using it to wipe the sweat from his forehead. His jaw was tense and I noticed he was refusing to look at me.

'Stay here,' I said, dropping my bag next to his. I could see ahead that the path and fence took a sharp right and I wanted to see what was around the corner. When I got to the turning, noticing how easy and buoyant my body felt walking without the bag, I saw that just to the side there was a space where the dirt road cut into the fence line towards a gate so that farmers could access the pomegranate field. It wasn't ideal being on a track that a car might potentially drive down, but it was late in the day and thus unlikely to be used, plus the space was flat, mostly free from gravel and brambles, and big enough for the tent. It would do.

Once unpacked we both changed out of our clothes and I hung them on the fence to dry. We were each carrying two sets of clothes with us, one for hiking and the second for resting and sleeping in. My resting clothes consisted of my favourite NASA T-shirt and a pair of thin, baggy red trousers. Although it felt good to take off the hiking clothes, which were saturated in dust and sweat, I knew it was unlikely they'd fully dry overnight. I was already dreading the moment I had to put on the same smelly, slightly damp clothes the next morning.

'Are you hungry?' Gil shook his head. 'Me neither, although we should probably have something small before bed.' An idea came to me and I jumped up, grabbing one of my walking poles. Twisting it so it was at its maximum length, I held the pole from the bottom and fed it through one of the squares in the fence. Then, easing it towards the nearest pomegranate tree, which was just too far from the fence line for any greedy hand to be able to reach, I slowly coaxed the handle of the walking pole around a huge pomegranate before tugging it with force. It popped free from the tree and rolled towards me close enough that I could reach down and grab it through the fence. Using a penknife I cut it open and we both started scooping seeds into our mouths. It seemed impossible that something so sweet and juicy could grow in such a dry place.

We were only part way through gorging on the fruit when the sound of a large engine interrupted us. We both looked up as a military helicopter appeared right above the fence line and soared over our heads. I covered my ears and yelled out when the roar of the engine cut through my body, the bass jarring my ribcage and vibrating my organs. It continued on to the space where all the dead brambles were just in front of us but then stopped and hovered just ten metres above the ground. By this point we were being hit by a powerful wind that threw a tornado of sand, sticks and brambles right towards us. Sensing a hot night ahead, we'd only put the inner netting of our tent up, not bothering with the waterproof nylon outside layer. The tent, held up by our lightweight poles, was now bending at a precarious angle. I unzipped the door and leaped in, pushing my hands against the side of the tent to right it against the strong winds, worried the poles could snap any minute. Gil jumped in after me, grabbing with him on the way a few of our possessions, which were being blown about, then zipped up the tent behind him. Although the netting was stopping some of the larger pieces of debris from hitting us, we were still being hammered by sand and thorns, making it hard to breathe or open my eyes. I pulled my T-shirt up over my face.

'They don't know we are here!' Gil yelled above the noise, also shielding his face with his T-shirt. I realised that where we had camped, up against the fence, we were completely obscured from their view.

I stuck my hand out of the tent door and waved it frantically, trying to catch the attention of whoever was flying this massive machine, although it was facing the other way. The helicopter was still hovering just off the ground, twisting left and then right, almost teasingly, until it finally turned a full 180 degrees and faced us head-on. The second it did, it shot straight up in the air and sped off the way it had come. My ears were ringing in the loud silence that followed.

'I guess they finally saw us, then.' I looked across at Gil who was so covered in dust that his black hair was now completely white. He shook his head and a cloud lifted from him. I ran my hands through my own hair, which was knotted and dishevelled, and then along my face, which felt like sandpaper under all the grit.

We tried to shake off as much of the sand as we could from our sleeping bags and clothes. Thankfully, the fence had acted as a net, scooping up the few items we had missed. I desperately wanted to wash but we had just two litres of water between us which we needed to preserve until our next filling station, a seven-kilometre walk away. I made do with a swig to rinse the worst of the debris from my mouth. How ironic, I thought, that I'd been making an effort to brush down my clothes and items once in a while to keep the dirt off!

As soon as the sun set on the horizon a surprising chill hit the air and we retreated to our tent. It felt wrong going to bed so filthy, lying down on the roll mats with bits of grit rubbing against my skin. It hadn't even reached 8pm before Gil nodded off next to me. I watched him silently, studying his face, now soft with sleep, and the freckles on his nose which already seemed more prominent, while I tried to take in all the drama of the last two days. I knew walking the trail would be hard but this had been more than either of us had imagined, and it was all my fault. This was my idea.

Chapter 2

Sighing, I turned over, pulling my sleeping bag over me like a blanket, and closed my eyes, trying to settle my uneasy mind, my thoughts stuck on a loop. There was no point thinking about it now. The only thing worth doing was closing my eyes and letting sleep take me. Making the most of the one time in the day when I didn't constantly fight with my my body to keep moving or my mind with the idea of quitting. If I thought hard enough, I could even convince myself that I was lying on a pillow, a soft duvet over me. That I was at home, the dusty trail nothing more than another fleeting idea that never quite came to be realised.

Chapter 3

'You're going to tell me we have to climb that, aren't you?' I said to Gil, who had stopped ahead of me. He looked at the map and then up at a very steep path which took a route up the side of the valley wall. I followed the path line up and could feel the burning in my legs and lungs already, anticipating the effort it was going to take to get to the top. It had been another hot and long day on the trail and, as we neared the end of day four of hiking, my energy levels were dwindling precariously.

Not only was this going to be a tough climb, but it was also what I had come to call Wasted Distance. We were in the middle of Nahal Amud Nature Reserve. The law in Israel allows wild camping anywhere except in nature reserves, where you are allowed to pitch only in designated camp areas. These spaces usually have no facilities, no toilets or running water, but act as a way of protecting the environment and containing human impact on the surrounding nature and wildlife. Tonight would be the first time we would test one of these camp areas and it just so happened that the camp was placed right at the top of the valley. We'd do this steep climb now, and then first thing in the morning we would have to clamber back down before rejoining the trail, and in the process would be no closer to finishing the 1,020 kilometres we were trying to cover.

Gil turned and held up his arms in surrender. 'It's a few hundred metres max, and once we are there we are done for the day.'

'Can't we just camp down here?'

'We can't. If a ranger catches us we'll be fined. Plus it's too rocky anyway.'

I groaned, knowing he was right and that I wouldn't have wanted to camp here anyway as I fully supported the concept of designated camping areas.

'The quicker we start the quicker it's done with,' Gil said, already starting up the path, scrambling over rocks and using his hands to help himself balance.

I followed behind, although wasn't able to match his pace. We'd been yo-yoing with our energy levels all day. Just as Gil's would dip I would find a burst. Now, with me struggling, Gil had suddenly found some hidden reserves. It seemed to work as a way of keeping us moving, with the more energised of us dragging the other along. If both of us had slumped at the same time there's a good chance we would have collapsed in a heap by the side of the trail and given up altogether.

After each big step I stopped for a few seconds to try to catch my breath and slow my pounding heart rate, before summoning the energy to drag my next heavy foot up. *I should have trained more*, I kept thinking. The intention had been there but, as always, I'd found excuses not to exercise until it was too late.

My frustration with myself was only making the climb worse and with each step my spirits slipped away, along with the small bits of gravel that tumbled down below as we disturbed them.

It took forty long minutes to catch up with Gil, who was waiting for me at the top of the climb. The map had promised a spring but, instead of the natural oasis I had been imagining, we were greeted with nothing but a dumping site. This was obviously a popular hang-out thanks to a single off-road track that led to the nearest city of Safed.

Piles of litter occupied the ground and bits of plastic, caught in the trees and shrubs around us, flapped in the wind. The spring was contained in a small manmade pool surrounded by concrete walls covered in graffiti. It gave the impression of a dodgy underpass that you wouldn't want to walk through, let alone sleep near. The camping area was laid out among ancient olive trees, their meandering branches and knobbly trunks giving each one a unique character. They looked sad in this setting of waste and manufactured detritus, demonstrating perfectly the need for these designated areas.

Despite the state of the place it clearly wasn't just a hang-out for youths. There was an older man sat on a blanket with, I assumed, his grandchildren, and a short couple wearing hats and heavy knitted cardigans, clearly oblivious to the heat. The man was swinging a broomstick at the tree trying to rid it of its olives and the lady was shuffling around bent over, scooping them up with blankets into buckets.

This sudden reminder of human existence was a stark contrast to the natural wonders we'd been rewarded with up to this point. The terrain in the north of Israel had not been what I was expecting, each day presenting me with scenery that made the task of hiking considerably more bearable. We'd been up and over mountains – small mountains, but big enough still to offer a view at the top worth pausing for. The first of the day had even taken us above the clouds; in the distance you could just make out Mount Hermon, at 2,814 metres the highest mountain in the region, its peak just visible floating on a sea of white.

We'd hiked along winding wooded tracks and, earlier that day, precariously made our way along a narrow ledge above a gentle stream, the sound alone instantly cooling my body. I'd never imagined Israel would have so many trees but large chunks of our hike so far had been through forests. The trees looked different to the lush, softer ones I was used to back home, the green a deeper shade, the trunks more defined with features and the surrounding shrubbery sharper and more brittle. We'd also spotted lots of cacti, passing carefully so as not to get too near their spikes. The overall effect gave the forests an uninviting feel but there was also a strength in their existence and their ability to survive in such a harsh environment.

I'd been surprised to hear Gil explain that much of the land had historically been covered in native trees and shrubs. Agriculture, housing and war had resulted in widespread deforestation but when Jewish immigrants began establishing settlements in the late nineteenth century, and when the area was under British Mandatory rule, a change in attitude led to the increased protection of natural spaces. Since then, tens of millions of trees have been planted across the country, mostly in the north.

I began kicking aside discarded plastic bottles, food wrappers and plastic bags to make space for our tent. We'd picked a spot that was on the edge of the camping space, next to a particularly pretty olive tree and away from the other people, although it looked like they were all close to leaving anyway. I made my way to the spring to inspect it more closely, my nose instantly wrinkling. There was a slow trickle coming in from one end, but mostly the water was still, with some areas collecting green algae. I would never normally contemplate cleaning myself in water that was so smelly and stagnant but I could feel the dirt on me like a suffocating hand. With each splash on my face, some of the struggles that had built during the day washed away.

'The water's too stagnant for drinking,' I said, returning to Gil. We were down to our last litre and would need at least another four to get us to the next water point; our plan had been to use the spring. I was about to suggest that we see if anyone there had any water to spare when I noticed the older man already walking towards us.

'Are you hiking the trail?' he asked, after introducing himself as Steve.

'Yes,' I replied. 'Have you walked it yourself?'

'Only parts of it. I've been out with my grandchildren today doing some hiking. I recognise that accent – where is home?'

'London,' I said although thinking of the fact that we no longer had a flat, jobs or anything that tied us to the place, I wondered if it really was home anymore. 'I grew up in Basingstoke.'

He laughed and I raised my eyebrows.

'I actually lived in Basingstoke for a short time.'

'You did?'

'I'm a Londoner really, but was evacuated there during World War II. Did you like growing up there?'

I shrugged. 'I didn't love it, to be honest.'

Steve's question wasn't an unusual one. The commuter town of Basingstoke has a bit of a bad reputation. It's a town with many nicknames, from Doughnut City to Concrete Jungle to – the one most of my friends opted for – Boring-stoke. My indifference about the place was about as flat as the grey concrete view you get as you enter the town centre. It was going to school there that I had really hated, and the problem with not enjoying school is that it's a long journey to endure: fourteen years, to be precise. So it was not surprising that the second I hit eighteen I turned my back on Basingstoke and all associations I had with my time there, taking just a handful of friends with me.

'Do you live in Israel now?' I asked Steve after we'd talked some more about Basingstoke and he'd shared what it was like being an evacuee.

'Yes, this is home for me now. Life is good here. I like the lifestyle, the weather, the food and, of course, the people.'

I nodded, immediately assuming he must be Jewish and had made Aliyah, the process by which Jewish people move to Israel and are granted automatic citizenship.

'Before I forget, do you have any spare water? We're running low.'

'I've just got half a litre left, I'm afraid.' He returned to where his grandchildren were sitting and retrieved a bottle of water. 'Sorry I've not got more. I'll write down my number, though, and you can give me a call if there's anything you need. I can drive to you later tonight if you don't have any luck finding water. Or if you need help further along on the trail. Anything, any time.'

'Wow, thanks Steve,' I said, taking the bottle and the card that he'd scribbled his number on.

'That's really kind of you,' Gil said, leaning forward to shake his hand.

'No problem – and good luck!'

I watched Steve as he walked away with his grandchildren, wishing he would stay longer. The strange coincidence that we'd both called the same place home for a time made him an instant friend in an unfamiliar land.

The short couple had also now left, their buckets piled with olives. They had shaken their heads when we'd asked if they had water, leaving us on our own once more. Gil started scooping up our empty water bottles. 'I'm going to follow the stream back to see if I can find a clearer source.'

While I waited for Gil to return I sat by the base of the olive tree and pulled my rucksack towards me. We had opted for matching Thule fifty-litre rucksacks, although Gil had the men's version, black and grey, and I had the ladies' version, a not very attractive two-shade purple that made me think of the nineties. It was a simple bag with a large main compartment, a spacious pocket on the lid, and stretch pockets on the front and on each side – perfect if I wanted to stuff in water bottles or an extra layer of clothing for easy access. It had been hard trying to organise everything into our bags in such a way that we would be able to find items when we needed them, so we had taken the advice of a shop assistant who told us to use stuff sacks to separate all our gear. I'd initially been reluctant when I saw the cost of what seemed like yet another overpriced hiking accessory but had been converted. In my bag I now had a large stuff sack for my clothes, another for food and snacks, and then the 'bits and bobs' bag which held all the miscellaneous items including head torch, spare batteries, first-aid kit, penknife and the one phone that we had brought between us. They were each a different colour, making them easy to find, and had the added benefit of being waterproof, which I assumed also meant dust-proof.

I pulled out the yellow stuff sack, which contained our food rations, so that I could organise them for the next day. I had made a habit of doing this each night so I could separate the snacks, lunch and dinner so they were to hand, while also making sure we were rationing properly. It took a lot of discipline not to eat the food laid out in front of me. So wary of not carrying too much extra weight, we'd underestimated how much food we would each need to keep ourselves full. It seemed to be a fine balance: taking into account the weight of our supplies while also accepting that hunger pangs were likely to be our permanent companions, no matter how much food we had.

I did discover that we had some spare stock powder, which gave me the idea that I could make an improvised salty soup as an addition to our pasta dinner that night – assuming Gil could find some water.

The 4x4 police car was so quiet I didn't notice it until it was right in front of me, causing me to jump. The driver's window rolled down and a stern-looking policeman, wearing sunglasses, stuck his elbow out of the window and barked something at me.

'Sorry, I don't speak Hebrew,' I said, reaching for the map so I could show him that we were allowed to camp here. Maybe we'd misunderstood it and this still counted as the nature reserve.

'I said, you have drugs?' he repeated, this time in English with a dense Israeli accent.

'Oh. Um, no.'

'You've taken drugs?'

'No.'

'Are you sure?'

'Yes.'

'You are not lying?'

'No.' I lifted my hands up as if to show him they were empty. 'I've not taken any drugs and I don't have any drugs!'

'*Beseder*,' he replied, Hebrew for OK. The window started to roll up and the police car moved forward.

'Wait,' Gil called from behind me, jogging towards us, the bottles in his arms still empty. He exchanged a few words with the policeman and turned to me. 'They're going to take me to a gas station nearby so I can fill up with water.'

I was so confused by the brief drug interrogation that it hadn't occurred to me that they might be able to help us. Gil climbed into the back seat, a beaming grin now on his face. As they drove away from the campsite he turned and looked out of the rear window and gave me a big thumbs up, clearly excited about his ride in a cop car.

It was nearly an hour later when I started to worry that he hadn't returned. By this point I'd organised our food, finished making dinner, confident we would now have enough water, and had even returned to the spring for a second wash of my face. I'd tried reading but I kept wondering what was taking Gil so long and if I'd misheard him say that the gas station was nearby. Giving up on trying to distract myself, I instead stood by the tent looking around, hopeful for some clue.

My muscles instantly relaxed when I spotted the quad bike on the horizon. The driver was wearing an all-in-one white jumpsuit and a blindingly bright white helmet; behind him sat Gil, looking especially dirty in contrast, clutching the water bottles with one hand while the other gripped a handle behind him. The driver pulled up next to me and gave me a sharp nod of the head while Gil jumped off, letting the water bottles fall to the ground in a pile.

'*Toda raba*,' he shouted above the engine noise, thanking the quad biker who gave another sharp nod before revving and disappearing from sight at twice the speed.

'The police just left me!' Gil said, turning to me. 'They took me to the gas station and while I was filling up the bottles in the toilets they just drove off without saying anything. Bastards.'

'You're joking. Why would they do that?'

'They just don't care.'

'What was the story with that guy?'

'I waited by the road for ages trying to hitchhike with a car. Then I saw the quad bike, so called him over. He didn't want to give me a lift because he thought I might get his suit dirty, but eventually agreed as I promised I wouldn't touch him.' I shook my head laughing, perplexed by the strangeness of the last hour. I gave Gil's tense shoulders a quick squeeze before giving him a hug. I was thankful to have him back and to know he was safe.

'Don't let them bother you, they're just idiots. And at least we got the water. And you got a ride in a police car. And on a quad bike.'

'So random, but you're right, it was quite fun.'

Just the same as on previous nights, as soon as the last of the sun was gone, at around a quarter to seven, we entered the comfort of our tent, unable to resist the temptation of our cosy sleeping bags. About an hour into sleep, I was woken. I opened the door of the tent slightly and peered out. A few metres away from us were two men setting up their own tent and having a loud heated discussion in the meantime. My watch told me it was 10.30pm. It crossed my mind that maybe they weren't aware that we were inside the tent sleeping. I considered calling out to say 'hello' but didn't feel like holding a conversation in my sleepy state, so instead I zipped the tent back up and gave a few loud coughs which I hoped would highlight the fact that we were there. Their conversation continued without interruption.

Gil is a much heavier sleeper than I am but eventually the noisy chatting woke him too and, far less shy than me, he called out asking if they could keep quiet. Their volume lowered for a bit but then got louder and louder until it was back to the same level as before. I could not sleep, despite how tired I felt from the day and no matter how many items I put over my ears to try and block the sound. Gone midnight, I heard the zips of their tent door and sleeping bags. Just a few more exchanged words and they fell silent, and I drifted back off to sleep.

It felt like I'd only been asleep for a matter of minutes when the tent was filled with a bright light and the sound of dance music, which startled me awake once again. I sat up confused and looked at my watch: 3am. The music and lights cut out and I realised it had been a car. Like before, I peered out of my tent and this time saw a man, dressed in a suit and tallith, the fringed garment worn by Jewish Orthodox men. He made his way towards the spring and I noticed he was carrying a large book under his arm. I retreated back inside my tent, confused by the situation but not worried. Even if they were noisy, it was nice to have the comfort of other campers nearby. Soon after came the undeniable sound of someone jumping into the spring, before the start of repetitive chanting and splashing.

'What the hell is he doing?' I asked Gil at one point, when he'd turned over and let out a sigh next to me.

'Praying. The spring is probably sacred.'

'Sacred. That spring is sacred? And why is he doing this in the middle of the night?'

'No idea. Maybe to pray at a specific time.' Gil rubbed his eyes, just visible by the moonlight illuminating our tent.

'Surely he won't be able to keep this up much longer?'

Gil let out a single loud laugh in response.

I thought of the graffiti-covered spring littered with rubbish, and of getting up in the middle of the night to go swim in freezing water near a camping spot. I tossed and turned, checking my watch repeatedly as I counted the minutes pass by. The chanting came and went in crescendos and I was finding it impossible to switch off from the noise.

'Can we just leave? Neither of us are sleeping,' I said. It was now 4am.

Dense with sleep deprivation, we packed down our tent, being quiet on the off-chance that the other campers were managing to sleep through the chanting, then switched on our head torches to start the demoralising climb down the valley to rejoin the trail. As we passed the spring, I kept my eyes firmly ahead, ignoring the stark-naked rocking body of the man holding up a Torah, his smartphone propped up on the side acting as a reading light.

Accounting for the steepness of the climb, and the fact it was dark, we took things slow. Even so, the way down felt much quicker at night when I could only see a short way ahead, or perhaps concentrating on not falling meant that I stopped noticing the passing of time. Either way, I was glad to be back on the trail an hour later with no more Wasted Distance to cover.

There were five kilometres to hike before we would be out of the valley and Nahal Amud Reserve. Even by torchlight, the valley was undeniably beautiful, although much of my attention was focused on scrambling over rocks and ducking under trees on the maze of the path that lay ahead. I scuffed my knees and knocked my head multiple times, my mind and body out of sync.

I resorted to using a technique that I had been using over the last days to keep myself going. Looking up, I saw a large rock by the side of the path. I made it my target to reach that rock knowing, with certainty, I had the energy I needed to get there. When I was in line with the rock I looked up again, picked out another feature, a boulder or a tree, and did the same again, blocking out any distance beyond the next marker I had set myself.

Head torches now stowed away, we waited for the sun to rise on the horizon, its light hitting the trees with a warm glow that woke the birds to a unified morning song. It was special being in a place so untouched and so early in the day when we could watch nature wake up long before most people had even made it out of bed for their morning coffee. It felt like we were the only people there, and perhaps we were. I tried to focus on that to get out of my hurting body but the turmoil of negativity was a constant chatter in my ear.

Later that day, we came to an outdated café, the first food stop since the convenience store three days before. I'd been daydreaming about the café all morning, pushing my legs as fast as they'd go, desperate to reach it, desperate for the next break. I made sure to keep myself from getting too excited just in case they were closed or didn't have a lot of food on offer. I needn't have worried, though. When it came into view, the first thing I saw was the sign promising falafel inside.

We both ordered the same: freshly baked round pitta bread stuffed with falafel, tahini, hummus and salad, with extra hummus and a plate of chips to go with it. As instructed, we took a seat in the poky space by the window and eagerly waited for lunch to arrive, the teasing sound of falafel sizzling in the cooking oil in the background. I flopped down into the chair, my muscles melting into the hard surface. I gave my shoulders a squeeze to try and release some of the tension, but they were too tender to touch so instead I crossed my arms on the table and rested my head on top of them, acknowledging just how tired I was. It was a weariness I'd never experienced. Every cell in my body was hurting and straining hard just to keep moving. The lack of sleep and my unpredictable emotions were leaving me fraught and sensitive. Surely this was my limit?

There were no other customers in the shop so it was just us and the three middle-aged men who worked there, one cooking our lunch behind the counter and the other two stood in front of it. They began arguing, distracting me from my own thoughts. The older of the three was getting louder and louder, his arms beginning to wave about in all directions like a disgruntled toddler. Within minutes it had become a full-blown shouting match.

'What are they arguing about?' I asked Gil.

'I'm not sure. They're mostly just shouting insults at each other. I think it's something to do with the older guy taking a lunch break that was too long.'

Our food was dished up into small plastic trays and the older guy paused from his shouting match to pick them up and bring them to our table, where he slammed them down hard right in front of my face without a word. I just ignored him, not able to concentrate on anything except the delicious food that was in front of me. After a few mouthfuls, I forced myself to slow down just a little so I wouldn't make myself feel sick; still, it was gone in minutes.

While Gil made the most of the café Wi-Fi and power socket, I got up to look at the shop attached to the café. It was only small, basically a glorified pantry, with stacks of tins and packets of food. I thought it could be worth picking up some extra snacks while we were here. The older guy from the café followed me into the shop and stood by the till while I browsed. Nothing had prices on. I picked up a bag of crisps.

'How much is this?'

'Do you want it or not?' he spat, arms crossed, not even bothering to look at me. I shoved the crisps back on the shelf and returned to our table, deciding we could go without.

'This is crap,' I said, sitting back down. Gil looked up from the phone but didn't say anything. 'This is really crap.'

'What is?' Gil said, now putting the phone down.

'Everything. I'm so tired. The trail is just relentless and then even the parts that are meant to be nice, like having lunch, are just not.'

'What happened?' Gil asked, looking across at the older worker who was now aggressively cleaning tables.

'Nothing.'

'Just ignore him, he's an idiot.'

'Can we go?'

'I'd like to stay a bit longer.'

'But the sooner we go the sooner we can get the bloody hiking done for the day.'

'I know that, but it's also nice to rest for a bit and to sit in an actual chair. Like I said, just ignore him.'

'I am ignoring him. I just want to get going already,' I said, causing Gil to sigh. 'It's easy for you to say,' I snapped. 'You aren't finding it so hard.'

'Not finding it hard? You know that's absolutely not true.'

'Well, I just feel like I can't do it. This is just beyond me.'

'Probably because your expectations are too high.'

'What's that supposed to mean?' I said, feeling my temperature rising slightly.

'I'm just saying that you beat yourself up a lot. You make it worse for yourself. It's exhausting. As if you haven't already got enough to deal with you're constantly thinking you aren't hiking fast enough, that you aren't good enough to trust your decisions, that we should have trained more.'

'We *should* have trained more.'

'I know.' Gil's voice was rising slightly. 'I know we should have. I'm annoyed at myself as well for that, but there's no point thinking about it now. That's just the reality.'

'And maybe the reality is I can't physically do it.'

'But you are doing it.' Gil raised his arms in frustration. 'I don't know why you can't see it. Sure, we aren't exactly fast or finding it easy. But we are doing it. We got this far, didn't we?'

I started to say something then stopped myself, feeling anger bubbling up inside me. I yanked my bag on and stormed out of the café. I purposefully didn't turn around but heard the door of the café open and then the click of Gil's sticks, so I knew he was following me.

Finding the next INT marker, I began making my way towards the 400-metre climb up Mount Arbel. I followed the winding switchbacks upwards. The path became steeper and rockier until I was scrambling, but I refused to slow my pace, feeling rage pumping through my body. I continued on like an angry bull, stubbornly refusing to turn around, all the while arguing with myself in my head. By the time the peak was in sight, silent tears had joined the sweat dripping off the end of my nose.

The ground flattened out and, for the first time, I looked up. The view took me so much by surprise that I stopped entirely just to take it in. Ahead was the Sea of Galilee. It was much bigger than I thought it would be, a silvery-blue lake bordered by mountains. The colours were so soft and the lake so still it almost didn't look real; it could have been a painting. Dotted around the lake were small settlements, the lights just starting to turn on at evening time. Like so much of the trail so far, the outside world was never far from sight, although it felt a million miles away.

At the top of Mount Arbel was a manmade viewpoint, a section cut into the side of the mountain. If we pitched our tent up against the mountain we'd be far enough from the edge to make it safe while also having the benefit of shelter from the wind and a view that people travel all over the world to see. I wiped away my tears using the sleeve of my shirt. Whether it was allowed or not, I was done for the day and this perfect shelter felt like a kind gesture from the trail.

Gil came and stood next to me, shoulders slumped under his rucksack, dark rings under his eyes, face glistening with sweat. He took in the view and then spotted the shelter.

'You think this'd be OK?' I said, knowing he was thinking the same as me.

'Yeah. I think it'll be just fine. We can just leave early.'

We set up camp and then sat by the tent leaning against the rock face, our feet out in front of us. Both as calm and quiet as the view.

'I'm sorry,' I said, leaning over and giving Gil a kiss on the cheek. 'I get it.' His stubble instantly irritated my skin. He had decided he wasn't going to shave for the entire hike. Gil lifted his arm and put it around me, instantly dropping everything, never one to hold a grudge.

I took a deep breath in and let it out with a sigh. My anger was not with Gil, with the grumpy guy in the café or with noisy campsites that were meant to be quiet and clean. It had nothing to do with the dust or the heat of the trail, with litter or lost turnings. I knew my anger was only with myself. With my need to compare myself to others and, by doing so, to set expectations too high.

I was red-faced, sweaty, lost, slow and clumsy but, damn it, I was walking this thing, still putting one foot in front of the other and that had to count for something.

'You know we passed a hundred kilometres?' Gil said, changing the subject.

'No. That's mad.'

'We passed it just before reaching the top of Arbel.'

'It's cool to say we've walked a hundred kilometres.'

'Not to mention with massive rucksacks on our back and in insane heat.'

'But not as cool as being able to say we've camped overlooking the Sea of Galilee.'

'That is true. This is really surreal. Cheers,' Gil said, lifting his Nalgene water bottle, which I lightly tapped with mine.

A gentle breeze blew away the last of the heat from my face. I'd spent so long wishing I was somewhere else but right now, for the first time since joining the trail, I didn't want to be anywhere but here.

Chapter 4

It was day nine on the trail. A new day, each morning a chance to start over with renewed enthusiasm and hopefulness. Focusing on the small wins felt easier than usual, because the day before had been the best one yet. The path had been mostly flat and the temperatures milder, coming in around the mid-twenties mark, that tiny dip in the thermometer reading making all the difference. Despite knowing that today offered us more challenging terrain and that the forecast wasn't in our favour, and the fact I intuitively felt that two consecutive good days on the trail was likely to be a rare occurrence, I was still feeling a light optimism. I was embracing the struggles more, not dwelling on the tough times, and practising being kinder to myself. I thought of the fact that we were just days from Zichron Ya'akov, Gil's home town, where we would take a rest day with his family. For a lot of the trail I really believed I would never reach it, not on foot at least. The town had seemed so far away, with too many kilometres between me and it, but now it felt tangible, safely within distance.

As I took those first steps, another thought also crossed my mind. Although my pack was still heavy, still rubbing my hips raw in that same painful spot and digging into my shoulder blades, my body was noticeably more conditioned to carrying the load. When I'd picked it up that morning, I didn't have the usual shock on feeling its weight or dread at the thought of carrying it for the day. The muscle memory in my arms knew what to expect and my legs and core knew how much extra work they needed to do to keep me moving forward. I'd managed to identify the bag adjustments that worked best with my body as well as perfecting packing so that the weight was better distributed. For the first couple of days on the trail, I'd woken in the middle of the night to intense pain shooting up my shoulders and neck, causing pounding headaches that only a strong dose of painkillers would ease. Packing the heaviest items, mostly the food and water, lower in the bag now meant the weight sat more on my hips and not on the upper part of my back, easing the pressure considerably. The bag was now an extension of my body, as recognisable as a limb, albeit one that sapped my energy only second to the heat.

In front of me, just visible by the beam of my head torch, the sun not yet risen, I could make out the shadows of Gil and Eitan, the youngest person we'd met yet on the trail, just seventeen years old, doing some hiking before joining the army. They were chatting quietly together while I purposefully hung back. Although I'm not usually one to turn down a conversation, I need defrosting time following an early start. Eitan loomed over Gil: tall, broad-shouldered, long-limbed and carrying some extra weight, he moved clumsily, a boy not yet familiar with this new body which had, no doubt, rocketed in recent years. As he walked he tripped every few minutes and I noticed one of his laces coming loose for the second time already that morning. On his back was a scruffy pack, considerably bigger than our own bags, with many items hanging off it attached by ropes and clips. He was completely bare except for a pair of socks, hiking boots and baggy blue-striped boxers.

We'd met Eitan the night before while staying in a large warehouse which had been marked on the online 'Trail Angel' directory for the INT. Trail Angel is the name given to anyone who helps hikers on the trail with anything from food, lifts or places to sleep. The owners of this particular farm had said hikers could stay in their warehouse when they passed through, free of charge. They had posted instructions on how to find it, noting it was likely there would be no-one there when we arrived.

It had looked like something from a horror movie. Perched in between empty farmed fields was the warehouse, a tin roof with open sides. Inside, the place was littered with farming equipment and scraps of metal. It if wasn't for the sign pointing hikers towards a working tap round the back, I would have believed we had stumbled upon the wrong place. I surveyed the space for somewhere we could lay out our mats and sleeping bags and opted for a large, slightly raised slab of concrete in the middle. The vibe of the place wasn't exactly inviting but the thought of not having to put up the tent and pack it away the next morning won over atmosphere. Eliminating this simple task from my day, which in total would take us no more than ten minutes, gave me such a feeling of gratitude.

I now had a routine firmly in place. As soon as my bag hit the ground I was at my feet, pulling at my laces and tugging off my boots and socks, which I would lay out to dry as much as possible before the morning. My sandals would go on and my wrinkled, swollen feet would sigh in the air and space. The sleeping gear and tent would go up first, before I pulled out the rest of the items we'd need for the night. Once organised, then came arguably my favourite part: changing into my night-time clothes. It elicited the same feeling as leaving the office for the last time before a holiday. A message that, for today at least, the grind of walking on the trail was done. I'd stretch, usually no more than a few token attempts at reaching my toes, falsely promising that I'd do more the next day, then set about boiling water for whatever was for dinner that evening. This simple evening ritual helped settle me each night and took the edge off sleeping in a new and unfamiliar place, which still made me nervous. There was always a part of me that could relax a bit more, though, once my sleeping gear was set up and I knew I had somewhere to sleep that night.

The warehouse came with the added luxury of a running tap, which meant I also included a wash of the face, pits and bits. I was bent over on my third attempt to wash the grime from the back of my neck, using a collapsible mug to splash water over me, when I heard voices approaching. Thankfully, I'd just put my top on, being a bit more discreet than usual as I was aware that farmers might have been checking on the fields. It hadn't occurred to me that we might be joined by other hikers. On our journey, we'd passed the occasional day hiker but mostly we saw no-one. Rounding the corner, though, two young men appeared, their large rucksacks indisputably indicating that they were also doing a multi-day hike. The boys, who had been deep in happy conversation, waved when they saw us.

'Hey! How are you? I'm Noah,' the taller of the two said, sporting a well-defined beard that was cut short like his hair. It amazed me that when Israelis saw me they could tell, just by looking at my pale skin and lighter hair, that they should opt for English – which is well understood in the country as one of the national languages, alongside Hebrew and Arabic. We all introduced ourselves, and we learned that his companion was called Amos.

'How long are you hiking the trail?' Gil asked.

'The whole way, maybe,' Noah answered while Amos headed off into the nearby fields to listen to heavy metal on his iPod, something he apparently did each night.

'Why maybe?' I said.

'I'd like to, but we're just going to see. If it stops being fun then I'll go home.' I envied the casual free pass he gave himself.

'I would have been home about an hour into day one then!' I laughed, although when Amos didn't reciprocate I instantly regretted saying it. I saw by the way they were joking when they walked up to us, barely a sweat on their brows, a lack of relief on their faces at finishing the day, that they were hiking a trail very different to mine. Both fit and strong, recent army leavers, accustomed to the heat, for them the hiking didn't seem to be nearly as much of a challenge.

'What do you mean?' Noah asked.

'We're not as fit as you guys,' Gil piped in. 'It's not been so easy for us.'

When Amos returned from listening to his music, they both began making dinner while we talked more about the trail. I wanted to know everything, what they'd seen, which day had been their favourite and which their least. I felt an instant bond with them, knowing they'd walked the same dusty path as us to this point. It had been such a big thing for me, such a huge undertaking, and, Gil aside, Amos and Noah were the first people I could properly share that with, even if our experiences had been very different.

Our dinner had been a simple affair of couscous with dried vegetables already mixed in. Amos and Noah, however, spent a fair bit of time preparing their food. From their packs they pulled fresh vegetables, including potatoes, onion and garlic, a tub of mixed herbs, tins of sardines, a small jar of oil and even a full-sized frying pan! They were cooking up a feast. I marvelled as they carefully sliced the vegetables using a penknife and salivated at the smells that filled the air. I thought for a moment that maybe we had been doing food all wrong, until I considered how heavy their bags must be.

After a week exchanging barely more than a few words with passing strangers, conversation flowed, from music tastes to differences and similarities between our countries. So engrossed was I in conversation and my interest in their lives, I didn't notice the light fading around us. I asked with genuine curiosity what the boys hoped to do now they had finished the army, and heard how they both planned to go to university, but hadn't thought much beyond that. It felt like such an important time in their life, the moment when you first encounter the endless crossroads in front of you and when the one you pick can determine the course of your life forever.

'Did you go to university?' Noah asked me.

'Yeah, I studied film.'

'You wanted to work in movies?'

'Not particularly. It crossed my mind for a while but mostly I just picked a subject I was interested in and thought I could do OK in.'

We all fell silent when we heard the sound of something approaching from the darkness outside, just beyond the reach of the dim warehouse lights. It sounded like the clang of a bell attached to a moving cow. It wasn't a cow, but Eitan who stepped into the light. Shocked at the sight of him walking naked apart from his footwear and boxers, no-one spoke for a few moments.

'Hey,' he said, much too loudly, raising a giant hand in greeting. I saw that the clanging sound came from the objects hanging from his bag – another frying pan!

'Hey!' we all said back. We watched as Eitan pulled a mess of items from his bag, talking about something that had happened earlier that day involving a car and a lost man, although I think none of us were able to keep up with the story. As he moved things about he kept dropping them with his stumbling hands, a bull in a china shop.

'Why the boxers?' Amos asked eventually, when there was a pause in Eitan's monologue.

'These pants are all you need for hiking. You get lots of air and they stop your legs from rubbing.' He pulled one leg of the boxer up to demonstrate the lack of rubbing and I looked away just in time, aware I was about to get a view of more than just his chafe-free leg. Eitan said he was planning on two weeks of hiking and, although I was fascinated to find out more about this gentle giant, I couldn't ignore the call for sleep any longer.

'I think I'm going to have to go to bed.'

'Me too,' Gil said, and I noticed for the first time how red and watery his eyes were. It was nearly 10pm, a full hour and a half later than we'd managed to stay up yet.

'Just to warn you guys we get up early, five-thirty am,' I said.

'So early?' Noah said, his tone of voice telling me he was using a statement to ask a question, something that Hebrew speakers often did.

'We like to do some of the day's hiking before it gets too hot. We're not as used to the heat as you guys. But don't worry, we'll be quiet.'

'I'll join you,' Eitan said.

'Are you sure? Do you usually get up that early too?' I said.

'No. But I have a big day tomorrow. I'm going to go off the trail to do some extra climbing.'

'OK, sure. We pack away quickly and don't stop for breakfast until we've hiked for a bit, though.'

'Me too.'

'Great.' I exchanged a knowing look with Gil. Probably when the alarm sounded on our watch Eitan wouldn't join us and, even if he did, he would probably take ages to get ready.

When the alarm did sound the next morning, I pulled out the rolled-up bits of toilet paper I'd stuffed into my ears predicting, correctly, that conversation would continue loudly even with us sleeping close by. To my surprise, Eitan was out and ready even before we were, although, to be fair, he did sleep in his hiking boxers so had fewer morning tasks to complete. By the time we were leaving the warehouse he was by our side, teaching me a lesson not to judge people too soon.

'Wait a second,' I called to Eitan, noticing the exaggerated slant in his rucksack. 'Your bag is leaning completely to one side; that must be really bad for your back.' I tried to adjust the left strap to pull the leaning side in but discovered it was jammed stuck.

'It doesn't bother me,' he said, shrugging his shoulders and continuing on.

By the time we reached the road, the sun was just minutes from making its first appearance of the day. Mount Tabor, a 575-metre freestanding mound protruding from the landscape, and its climb, was clearly visible in front of us, as was the orange, blue and white INT sign directing us straight to it. Eitan came to a stop to tie his shoelace again and almost overbalanced entirely under the weight of his bag, catching himself just in time. Standing up, he reached around to try to grab his water bottle, which was clipped to his bag. After a few failed attempts I unclipped it and passed it to him.

'I'm going to leave now,' he said between large gulps. 'I'm going to go this way first for a different climb before I go to Mount Tabor.'

'Are you sure? You can stay with us if you like,' I said.

'No, I'm good. I'll see you later.'

'OK, well be careful. And just in case we don't see you, good luck with the rest of your hike. It was nice meeting you.' I quickly stuck my hand out for a shake before any attempt was made at a sweaty hug with his naked body.

'I'll definitely see you again. I walk very fast.'

'I hope so,' Gil said, also shaking his hand.

We stood and watched Eitan as he made his way into the treeline, until all that was left was the sound of his clanging, breaking the otherwise peaceful morning.

'I worry about him hiking on his own.'

'Me too. He's going to break a leg,' Gil said, before turning on his heel and taking the next path on the crossroads towards Mount Tabor.

In the midst of the usual muscle burn I felt on any major ascent, my clothes sticky and wet with sweat, I resorted to my trusted technique, which had never failed. I found a tree in the distance and focused on getting my legs to walk towards it, blocking out all other thoughts and distances ahead. We were part way up the mountain, in among trees on a very steep track that seemed to be going on forever in endless switchbacks. I could see a clearing just ahead and powered my legs forward, thinking that must be the top. When I reached it, though, it turned out to be a false peak, the real one still a way to go.

I put out my hand to steady myself against a tree and tried not to get irritated by how quickly I'd moved from feeling strong and energised this morning to feeling tired and worn out. I pulled my MP3 player from my pocket. Before leaving for the trail I'd loaded it with a mix of playlists of all my favourite songs, as well as a few podcasts. It had proved a valuable tool in boosting my spirits. As opportunities to charge our devices were infrequent I had been selective about when to use it – most days I tried to save it for after lunch, when I was guaranteed an afternoon slump – but I desperately needed something to keep me going now, even if it was still only 8am. Opting for music, I turned the volume up to maximum and continued on until, at last, I reached the real peak.

The path under my feet very suddenly turned from gravel and dirt to pristine neat paving. I looked up and took in the Greek Orthodox monastery which had found its home on top of this sacred mountain, surrounded by well-kept gardens and grounds, full of straight lines too harsh after the forest we'd just walked through. The place was grand but eerily quiet. We made our way to the main building and stuck our heads inside the church. Other than a man wearing simple brown clothing, who I assumed was one of the pilgrims staying there, it was empty. I studied the intricate and extravagant designs on the celling, noticing the sound of sung prayers in the distance.

It had taken us much longer to reach the top of Mount Tabor than we had anticipated, so we didn't hang around long before carrying on. After such a gruelling climb I was looking forward to an easy – or so I thought – downhill. Leaving the squeaky-clean monastery behind and stepping back on to gravel, I saw that the path dropped steeply downwards. Taking a few tentative steps, I felt my boots slipping on the loose rocks, causing my legs to tense. I turned my feet sideways and began slowly shuffling down, one step at a time, while using my left hand to grab on to tree branches or rocks as a backup just in case I did slip. Gil, who was much more confident on the downhill sections, skied ahead of me, using the loose gravel in his favour to glide down the mountainside. I tried to copy his confident stepping but as soon as I lost control I instinctively tensed, reaching out for something to help me stop.

It left me with no option but to continue my slow sidestep shuffle, meaning that by the time I reached the bottom my core muscles were stiff from all the tensing. It had taken an exhausting effort to get up and over Mount Tabor, but it had accounted for nothing more than five kilometres. This was going to be a tough day. I braced myself for the distance we still faced, my prediction that two good consecutive days on the trail was unlikely already proven true.

* * * *

The heat pounded down on my sun hat and my shirt collar, which was pulled up high to protect my pale skin from the rays. I was hot, so hot that my vision kept going fuzzy and blurring at the edges. It was making me feel sick and no amount of water helped ease my parched mouth or soothe my dry, cracked lips. I tried to imagine what the chill from the morning had felt like, when I'd started walking with a fleece and beanie hat on, but it was hard to grasp how it could ever have been cool enough for extra layers.

I was carrying most of my water in what is called a hydration bladder: a flexible plastic pouch that holds up to three litres of water and easily slots into a specially designed pocket in my rucksack. The hydration bladder comes with a tube which feeds through the top of the bag and clips on to the shoulder strap. It was great for ensuring I sipped water little and often, the most effective way to stay hydrated, as it was easy to use and didn't involve having to get anything in and out of my bag each time I wanted to drink. The downfall of storing water this way, though, was that I had no idea how much I was drinking or how much I had left of my supply. As I paused to take another sip from the bladder it made a gargling sound and no water came. I'd finished it completely. It was only early afternoon and it was meant to last me to the end of the day. I reached around and grabbed the Nalgene water bottle which I carried in my side pocket. I'd drunk from it at lunchtime and there were just a few gulps left.

Gil stopped ahead of me as if he'd heard my thoughts. 'How much water do you have left?'

'Not much.'

He was also sucking on his bladder. 'I'm completely out. Crap! We should have filled up at the monastery.' We had both been lazy. Following the climb neither of us had wanted to face the effort of taking off our packs, pulling out the bladders and refilling them.

'I've got a bit left,' I said vaguely. 'You don't have any more in your Nalgene bottle?'

'No. Nothing.'

We'd picked a bad day to make such a stupid mistake. It was the hottest day yet, with temperatures soaring way into the thirties, higher than the forecast had predicted. Gil wiped his brow and looked out across the dry hills around us as if hoping a tap or water source would magically appear. We were about a forty-minute walk to the nearest house but it was in completely the wrong direction. Growing up in Israel, Gil had a better understanding of just how dangerous heat and lack of water can be and had told me of a friend of his who had died of heatstroke during a military exercise. It was to be expected walking in these temperatures that we would experience heat exhaustion and all the symptoms that come with it, from excessive sweating, nausea and headaches to appetite loss and cramps. If this isn't treated and monitored carefully, though, it can quickly turn to heatstroke, a much more dangerous condition that can kill a person in minutes. The best treatment for heatstroke is to submerge the body in water to cool its temperature. That is the biggest irony, of course, as in most cases it is a lack of water that brings it on in the first place. I was not showing any of the signs – not sweating, feeling delirious and shortness of breath – but being so far from water sources made me nervous.

We discussed our options and decided that we would push on, completing the last eight kilometres of the day to where there would be a large supermarket waiting for us; hopeful, though, that we would pass someone before then.

Ignoring the powerful need to quench my thirst, I tucked the water bottle safely back into the side of my bag and fell in behind Gil's footsteps. We both knew there was no point talking about it anymore, we just needed to keep moving. There was a tension in our hiking as the knowledge that we were so low on water hung over our heads. All we could do was shuffle forward and do our best to stay in the shade when it was available, usually when trees lined the path. At a snail's pace, we reached the peak of another climb, Mount Deborah.

'I need a break,' I said between breaths, blinking heavily from the sweat that had poured into my eyes and caused them to sting. There was a perfectly placed bench and a memorial plaque declaring that it was in honour of the twenty-fifth wedding anniversary of Queen Elizabeth II and Prince Philip. It seemed a strange thing to commemorate with a bench in what seemed like a random, albeit pretty, spot. I was grateful for its existence, though.

'Can you smell that?' Gil asked, dumping his pack on the bench next to me. I took a deep breath, also recognising the smell of weed. Gil was already in action tracking down the source, which came from two teenage boys on dirt motorbikes who had also chosen to stop for a break at the royal memorial.

'It's all they had,' Gil said, returning to the bench with about half a litre of very warm water in a battered plastic water bottle. The boys had already driven away, clearly startled that we'd caught them smoking. I looked at the water and thought how easily I could finish it in one gulp.

'There's about seven kilometres left to walk,' I said. 'One more big climb and then the rest is downhill to the supermarket. Let's take a big sip now, then see how far we can go before taking another one.'

'Sounds good.'

'You go first.' I handed the bottle to Gil.

'It's also four o'clock, so at least the worst of the day's heat should have passed. It'll only get cooler from now.' Gil took a sip before passing it back to me.

The swig of water did nothing to ease my thirst; in fact it only seemed to intensify it, a teasing reminder of what I was being deprived of. I was learning the hard way that laziness was not an option on the trail. Small problems very quickly developed into big ones if you didn't tackle them straight away.

'Don't worry, we'll be fine,' I said, noticing how worried Gil was looking.

'Of course we will. I'm just annoyed. We should have filled up at the monastery while we had the chance.'

'We didn't know it was going to be this hot.'

'We still shouldn't have taken the chance.'

'I know. There's no point dwelling on it, though, so let's just keep moving. The quicker we get there, the quicker we drink.'

The next hours melted into a blur, although at the same time I felt acutely aware of each step and each minute that passed. I pushed aside any complaints from my body, focusing only on our goal to reach the supermarket. My nausea increased and we both complained of headaches starting to develop. At the point I was sure we couldn't go any further and needed to call for help, the large concrete rectangle of the supermarket came into view.

I stuck my head under the tap and gulped and gulped at the cool water until my stomach gurgled from the liquid and I felt I might be physically sick. I cupped some water in my hands and splashed it on my face. Looking at the small cracked mirror in the supermarket toilet I could see the red raw skin on my cheeks and nose, the top layer already peeling in some areas. The sweating and heat had made futile my endless efforts to keep topping up with factor fifty-plus suncream. It had been a brutal day and all I wanted to do was curl up, preferably on a slab of ice, and sleep.

We threw our bags in a trolley and wandered the supermarket like zombies, grabbing at items and throwing in more food than we could eat. Before going to the checkout, we returned to the toilets for a second round of gulping down water. With the comfort of knowing our bottles and hydration bladders were now filled to the brim, we crossed the supermarket car park and entered a small wooded area. There had been plans to take a bus to the nearby city of Nazareth to spend the night in a budget hostel but it was now dark and neither of us had the energy to keep our eyes open much longer. I had wanted to see Nazareth, but it would need to wait for another day.

The wooded area was littered with empty beer cans and signs of fires, and the roar of a busy motorway hummed in the background. Already I was feeling that I just wanted this night to be over with and to be away from this place. We tried to find a discreet spot, hidden by bushes, and hoped that, with it being midweek, we wouldn't run into any trouble.

The walk to the supermarket had been along a narrow trail that was overgrown with spiky bare plants that scratched at my legs and embedded my skin with thorns. After using the tweezers from my penknife to pull some of them out, I crawled into bed.

Dinner was eaten in my sleeping bag. I didn't even have the energy to sit up, and we made only a small dent in our purchases. The rest would be eaten for breakfast. I was fraught and drained and couldn't even contemplate the thought of having to get up the next morning and start walking again. I clung to the knowledge that each day I woke amazed by how quickly my body had recovered, always less achey than I thought I would be.

We both snuggled down into our sleeping bags, listening to the call to prayer that was just audible, blasting through poor-quality speakers some distance away. I thought of Eitan and wondered why we hadn't seen him again. I hoped he had been OK in the heat. I thought about us running out of water, about the fine line between taking risks and being stupid. How one good or bad decision can change the course of your life forever.

'I just remembered,' I said, turning off the light on my head torch and plunging us both into darkness. 'You know what day it is today?'

'Mmmm?' Gil sounded next to me.

'Our anniversary. We met exactly six years ago today.'

Gil didn't reply. He was already asleep and, before I even managed to take the torch off my head, I had joined him.

Chapter 5

A full bladder woke me from a deliciously heavy sleep. There was one thing I had learnt very quickly on the trail, where rehydrating in the evening meant an unavoidable trip to the toilet in the middle of the night, and that was to go the second the thought crossed my mind. Holding it in leads to nothing but a prolonged disruption of sleep. Eventually, no matter how long I ignored my full bladder, I would have to give in, wishing by now that I'd just gone straight away. So, no matter how much I wanted to stay in bed, it was time to move.

The problem was that I had no idea where I was or where I should go for my night-time pee. My eyes were wide open but it was dark, too dark. I couldn't even make out my hands in front of my face.

I put out a hand to feel for the tent wall to search for the zip on the door but was confused to find nothing but air. Sitting up, I realised I wasn't on a roll mat but a foam mattress.

'What's wrong?' Gil stirred in his sleep next to me.

'I'm trying to work out where to go for a pee.'

'Um. Just use the toilet next door,' he replied, sounding as confused as I felt. The fog of sleep started to lift, memories from the night before coming back to me.

We'd made it to Zichron Ya'akov.

'It's alright, go back to sleep,' I said, stumbling out of bed before walking head first into the door, which I thought was open, causing me to laugh.

'What are you doing?'

'Sorry, sorry. Go back to sleep,' I repeated, still laughing to myself as I finally made it into the corridor.

It had taken a mammoth hiking day to reach Zichron Ya'akov. We had decided to set ourselves the ambitious task of arriving a day early, meaning we could squeeze in two full rest days. It meant covering forty kilometres in one go, fourteen kilometres more than we had managed yet in a day. We barely spoke all day, focusing on nothing but the task ahead. We passed picnic areas, full with families enjoying the weekend. We crossed through my favourite town yet, Ein Hod, made up entirely of creatives who had all been interviewed and selected to live there. Everything was a work of art in Ein Hod, from the drinking fountains to the benches and the street lamps; large sculptures dotted the pavements, and houses, converted to art studios, were open to the public. We casually hiked past a place of phenomenal historical significance, Nehal Me'arot, caves containing evidence of more than half a million years of human activity.

The trail was a rollercoaster of teasing ups and downs. The adrenaline kept me going until the last hour when my muscles started to seize up and the pain in my bruised and battered feet began to become unbearable as I hobbled ahead of Gil on the loose, rocky path. There was no way we were giving up at that point, though, not when we were so close.

Amir had come to meet us to drive us back to the house. Turning the corner and seeing his car, I had to bite my tongue to hold back the tears. He clapped as we limped up to him, giving us both a hug despite our grim state. He took us home, windows rolled down to ventilate the car from the smell of our feet, now escaped from their boots. As soon as we were through the door, I headed straight for the shower, where I watched the swirl of mud make its way down the drain as I soaped myself for the second time and then dried myself with a real towel. Mira cooked us a feast of which I had three, maybe even four, helpings. I managed barely half a pint of Goldstar, a popular Israeli lager, before I found myself crawling into bed.

Waking up the next morning I stayed in bed soaking up the knowledge that we now had two days of rest ahead of us, forty-eight full hours that I could fill exactly as I wanted. I lay still, staring at the walls for a while. Like the rest of the house, Gil's room was white and mostly bare, with high ceilings and hard tile floors. The main purpose of houses in Israel seems to be to stay cool so that the inhabitants can survive the harsh temperatures of the summer in relative comfort. This, along with the open-plan style of the living spaces and the bomb-shelter room on the ground floor, which was mandatory in all buildings, left the house feeling a little stark. However, despite the harsh interior I'd always felt at home here. It was a house where feet could rest on coffee tables and spoonfuls of dessert could be eaten straight from the fridge.

After breakfast, we decided to prioritise sorting out what we were now referring to as 'hikers' chores', so they were out of the way. This included washing our clothes, restocking our food supplies and catching up on emails. We also had a proper sort through our bags, taking the opportunity to leave behind anything that we hadn't been using and didn't want to carry any more. Gil joined me in his bedroom and we pulled everything out of our rucksacks, laying them neatly on his childhood bed.

There is nothing in my life that has been fabricated without a list. Preparation for the Israel National Trail was no different and, of all of them, it was the the What To Pack list that caused me the most stress. The outdoor stores, with their endless brands and mass of gadgets, were confusing places for a novice like me, so each item had been carefully researched, trusting the reviews of others online who knew what they were doing far more than I did, until we had gathered all the gear that we thought we would need.

We slowly sifted through all the items. If something hadn't been used yet we decided if we really needed to keep it with us. I was proud that my list and planning had paid off, as just six things were pulled out to be left behind: spare clothes that we could cope without, our waterproofs which hadn't been touched once, and my penknife, as we realised there was no need for us to carry two.

Heading downstairs and back to the fridge, where I knew I would find the foods I was craving most, anything fresh and cool, I bumped into Mira. She threw her arms up in the air and embraced me.

'Bexi,' she said, using the endearing name the family had christened me. 'You know we are so proud, right?'

Out of the corner of my eye I caught Gil giving me a warm grin. I'd been showered with compliments from his parents and I knew how much this meant to him. Being with someone from a different country always comes with challenges, including visa restrictions, one side being torn from their home and a mixing of cultures that doesn't always go smoothly. It had been difficult for everyone involved when Gil had moved abroad so that we could be together, leaving his family, who are very close, and it had taken some time, on all sides, to accept it.

Gil to me was always the man I had met aged twenty-two. I'd gotten to know him as a free-spirited explorer in the setting of Central American volcanoes and backpacking bars. I had no context for who he was before I met him other than the stories we shared about our lives late into the night or on long bus journeys as we travelled. It was when he was with his family, or on the few occasions I visited Israel, that the differences in our upbringings and cultures became most obvious. It made me appreciate what moving to the UK had really meant for Gil. He had to learn the intricacies of British mannerisms, such as the way people say 'thank you' and 'please' more than is necessary and often don't say what they really mean. It was a long while before he could watch a comedy sketch and understand all the references, or be at a party where he wouldn't feel lost in the conversation. Equally, I had to adapt to Israeli bluntness in order to mould into his family and to realise that Gil wasn't being rude when he simply, without any hesitation, spoke with absolute truth. I learned about the many Jewish celebrations and how to handle sensitive subjects like mandatory army service, the Holocaust and the Israel/Palestine conflict, which always cropped up when people learned I was married to an Israeli, no matter how much I tried to avoid them. Sometimes our cultural differences verged on the comical. Not least the day I'd first met Gil's family, all those years earlier. Excited after experiencing his first ever Christmas in the UK, Gil had convinced me that I should bring Christmas crackers, and that they would be the perfect gift. 'They'll love them much more than a box of biscuits,' he had insisted. Thus, I sat at the table on a sunny January day with my future Jewish in-laws, Mira, Amir, and Gil's younger brother Amit, with paper hats on their heads. Amit asked me, while turning over a pointless plastic jumping frog in his hands, what the meaning of a Christmas cracker was. It was a good question, to which I had no reply. In time, Gil and I melted into each other's ways, becoming a unique mix of both cultures, me a bit more Israeli and Gil a bit more British, taking the best parts from both.

'I know you are,' I said, pulling back from Mira's hug.

'I still can't believe you are here doing the hike. It's incredible,' Mira said to us both, rolling her eyes towards the ceiling as if she was taking in something impossible.

'Me either. I mean, before I met Gil I couldn't even pinpoint Israel on a map.'

'Really?'

'Yes, really. I honestly didn't know anything about the place.'

'And now you are hiking its full length, seeing more of the country than most people who live their whole lives here will see,' Gil added.

'Maybe. I'd never really thought of it like that before,' I said, before Amir appeared by my side, arms out in another proud embrace. I'd never get used to this level of hugging.

With all our hikers' chores done there was nothing left but to enjoy the sweet taste of rest and the knowledge that we'd made it to Zichron Ya'akov, a point I thought we would never reach. The town sat 250 kilometres into the trail, a quarter of the distance of the full INT. It was in both parts uplifting and demoralising. Uplifting because it sounded like such an impressive distance. Demoralising because it had taken so much for me to get this far that all that effort for just a quarter of the reward seemed unimaginable. We had made it, though, even completing a forty-kilometre day, something which I never could have done two weeks earlier when starting the trail.

I might not have seen it and I might not have felt it but changes were happening, progress was being made, and slowly, but surely, we were snaking our way south to the desert.

* * * *

Chapter two. That's what it felt like. The next stage of the trail. I could draw a line under the first part, put the ordeal, negativity and bruises behind me and look to what was next. It had not been easy starting back again that morning after two days off, Amir driving us to the exact point he had picked us up, but it was made more bearable because this was an especially exciting chapter to look forward to. I'd been eagerly anticipating this part from the beginning.

A stray black cat jumped from behind the bins and ran across my path, bringing with it the sharp, rotting-waste smell of the alley it had come from. A few steps further and this was replaced by the smell of Arabic coffee and freshly baked pitta bread coming from a bakery across the street.

'Shall we get some fresh pitta for our lunch?' I said, unable to resist the smell despite being uncomfortably full from breakfast.

'You read my mind. I'll get them.' Gil said before crossing the street and shuffling through a group of weathered-faced men stood outside the bakery smoking and drinking coffee from small glasses.

A car was parked right up on the pavement, blocking my way, so I stepped into the road to go around it and then perched myself on a crumbling wall in front of a courtyard filled with discarded bricks and rubble while I waited for Gil. I spotted a boy watching me from an ajar front door of a block of flats. Skinny, with dark skin and huge saucer eyes, he peered at me half-hidden by the door frame. He wore baggy, thick joggers and a sweatshirt despite the fact I was too hot in just shorts and T-shirt. I smiled at him. He gave me a coy grin then retreated back inside.

The mismatched, disorganised streets and the mosque with its domed roof told me that Jisr az-Zarqa was an Arab village. The Israeli/ Palestinian conflict is ever evident in Israel's towns and villages, which – apart from a few examples of blended multicultural neighbourhoods – are almost entirely segregated. Gil's home town, predominantly

Jewish, looked more Mediterranean in style compared to the Middle Eastern feel of Arab places like this. That said, all towns in Israel, regardless of the beliefs of their inhabitants, seemed to be centred around the same things: places of worship, fresh food and coffee.

As we continued through Jisr az-Zarqa I spotted signs of what I was eagerly awaiting. Battered boats left on trailers, large tangles of fishing nets strewn beside the pavements, a seagull flying overhead. I stepped on to the sandy beach and gazed out across the blue water ahead, so vibrant it looked like someone had bumped up the saturation on a photo. I felt a pull to strip off and jump in straight away but restrained myself, knowing the time for that would come later. Gentle waves slapped the sand at a lazy pace and my hair lifted in the ever so slight breeze. It was just a whisper of wind but enough to take the edge off the blazing heat. My shoulders dropped slightly. I smiled and took a deep breath. Gil raised his arms and walking poles up above his head, eyes closed, before turning to me and returning my huge smile.

We made our way along the beach, passing fishermen from the nearby villages, ducking under their lines, learning quickly that the best place to hike was on the wetter sand, recently washed by the waves and much more compact than the dry sand that swallowed up our feet. Straight away, I knew this was going to be as good as I had hoped. For three full days the sea would be our hiking companion, the trail following the coastline south until it reached the bustling city of Tel Aviv. From there, it cut inland east towards Jerusalem. The next time we'd see the sea again after that would be at the end of the hike, when we reached Eilat.

It meant that, apart from the occasional cliff climb, the path for three days would be entirely flat. The willpower I constantly had to tap into to get me up and over climbs was taking a short holiday.

The other big advantage was that there was space for Gil and me to walk side by side; normally, the narrow gravel tracks forced us to walk one behind the other. This, combined with our uplifted mood from being on the beach, a place we both loved, meant we spent much of the day chatting. I was so lost in conversation that I barely noticed the hours slipping by or the sun arching across the sky.

'This could be a good spot,' Gil pointed to a mound that sat back from the lapping waves, far enough that the high tide wouldn't reach it.

'We're at the end already?' We'd recently got into the habit of taking turns to shoulder the responsibility of navigating and keeping track of where we were on the map, and today was Gil's day.

'Yep. If we go any further we'll reach Hadera, so if we want to camp on the beach this is our last chance.'

We walked over to the mound to check the top was flat enough. If it wasn't for the trail of multicoloured microplastic pollution, a feature which had followed us all day, it would have been paradise.

Our tent was up in record time and I was first to strip down to my underwear. I ran towards the sea while Gil stayed behind to guard our stuff. There weren't many people around, just the odd dog walker and fisherman, but we didn't want to take the risk, especially with our tent, which was one of the most expensive things we owned. It had cost us over £300.

I took three big strides into the water and then fell back, letting a wave catch my weight. It was surprisingly warm but still delightfully refreshing. I floated on the surface for a minute but when I turned around I spotted the distinct white shape of a jellyfish floating not far from me. I hadn't swum in the sea many times in my life and the thought of being stung by a jellyfish freaked me out a fair bit. I waded away from it, relaxing back again until I spotted another even bigger jellyfish, and then another and another.

'That was quick,' Gil said to me back at the tent.

'The sea is full of jellyfish,' I said, picking up the thin shawl which so far had been used as a scarf, picnic blanket and towel.

Gil tore off his shirt and started making his way to the sea.

'You aren't afraid of them?' I yelled after him.

'They don't bother me.'

'What if you get stung?'

'That's what pee is for,' he called back before disappearing from earshot.

Sunset had turned the splattering of clouds a spectacular pink and I reached for our camera to take a picture of Gil in the sea against the vibrant sky. I then dug my feet in the sand and took the biggest breath I had taken yet on the trail. It was a breath of relaxation and satisfaction brought by an uneventful day of hiking alongside the ocean, a place where I instantly felt happy. I couldn't understand why I hadn't made more of an effort to spend time by the sea when I loved it so much, but knew that going forward that would change. Completing a day on the trail with ease gave me a mild sense of certainty. It was a mix of knowing how far we had covered and having a few easier days, reassuring me that it was the heat, heavy packs and terrain that made much of the trail so challenging and not just my inability to hike. Planning was now second nature, as was using all the equipment, tying up my boots in the morning and clipping up my bag securely. I followed the three-striped waymarkers with ease, knowing what pace to set to ensure we arrived at camp before dark while preserving as much energy as possible. What footing to choose for the most stable of steps on uneven ground. The trail was no longer a stranger but an old friend and I, at last, was worthy of my status as a long-distance hiker.

* * * *

We were nearing the end of our second day following the coastline and the beaches were getting busier as the distance between us and Tel Aviv closed. The combination of soft, flat sand beneath us and the sound of gentle waves had resulted in a great night's sleep. In fact, it had been the best night's sleep yet.

Gil was listening to a podcast, a whodunnit series about a real-life murder. We were taking it in turns to listen to it one episode at a time before having a debrief to discuss who we thought was guilty based on the latest evidence we'd heard. We were careful not to binge on it in one go, aware that the minimal entertainment we had with us had to last for two months.

The beach was a hub of human activity. People of all ages were there to swim and run, to do yoga or tai chi. Groups sat around sunbathing and eating, playing volleyball or *Matkot*, a popular bat-and-ball game that I'd often heard Israelis claim was their national beach sport. It was as interesting as watching animals in a zoo, although it crossed my mind that we were probably the most fascinating creatures there, with our walking poles, big packs and hiking gear, looking vastly overdressed compared to everyone else in swimwear.

Ahead, I saw tall fences blocking off a large rectangular section of the beach, about the length of a small football pitch. I stopped and waited for Gil to catch up with me so I could ask him what it was.

'It's the place where the Orthodox Jews go to swim in the sea or spend time on the beach. So the men and women can't see each other in their beachwear.'

Passing by, I noticed there were two entrances, one for women and one for men. I walked as close to the barrier as I could and in between the cracks in the fence could make out huddles of women in modest black swimwear. There are many different branches of Judaism, each with varying rules and levels of dedication. I was still discovering a lot of their quirks, many of them very peculiar to me. Like the restrictions around Shabbat, a day of rest marked between sunset on Friday to sunset on Saturday when religious Jews aren't supposed to expend any energy, even to the extent of not being allowed to press an electronic button. On that day elevators in Israel are often set to a 'Shabbat setting', whereby the doors will automatically open on every floor. It can make for a very tedious ride if you want to reach the top of a block of flats. It was for the same reason, Gil explained, that his friend had a basket full of torn-up tissues in his bathroom, because on Shabbat he isn't allowed even to tear toilet paper. I'd been embarrassed when I'd gone to shake the hand of his friend who explained he doesn't touch women.

As soon as we were past the structure, our pace slower because we had been wading through dry sand, we immediately returned to the water's edge. I spotted another structure that confused me: a big tent made of scaffolding tubes with rugs draped over the top. Music was blaring from the inside. Looking down the beach, I noticed it was littered with these makeshift tents of varying sizes as far as the eye could see.

'And what are they?'

'They're just tents that groups of friends or family build. They usually build them to keep up for the summer or for the holidays. Sometimes they stay in them overnight or just use them at the weekends or odd days.'

'And they're allowed to build these legally?'

'I think so, yeah.'

Peering inside the first one I saw thin mattresses laid out on the floor and a lot of tanned teenagers lounging about and drinking.

'I guess it's like the Israeli version of a beach hut,' I said, trying to see the positives and not just the pile of litter that had been dumped outside, blowing about in the wind.

'*Yalla, yalla,*' a man, coming from the next tent along, wearing only pink floral shorts and carrying a beer in his hand, shouted at us. Stopping midway, he waved frantically for us to come towards him. '*Yalla, yalla,*' which I knew to be an Arabic phrase meaning 'come on' or 'hurry up'.

We obediently walked towards him and he embraced us in a hug. I was self-conscious of my sweaty state although, judging by the stench of alcohol on his breath, I thought that he probably didn't notice.

'English? English?' he said to me, standing a little too close.

'Um, yes.'

'You walk the trail? Israel National Trail?'

'Yes, all the way to Eilat, hopefully,' Gil said.

'Good! Come, *yalla, yalla.*' He led us into the tent, which was much larger than the first we had seen. The set-up was quite impressive, with an array of seating options from sofas to beanbags, rigged lighting and a rusty fridge running on an audible generator. Just visible out the back, three coal barbecues were lined up next to one another, all smoking and crammed with a colourful selection of food. There were maybe twenty people in the tent, from children to a very elderly lady who sat in the corner drinking red wine from a plastic cup. The guy indicated for us to sit on a sofa and shoved a cold Goldstar, which he'd taken from the fridge, into our hands.

'We are all one family.' He waved his arms about enthusiastically. 'We do this every year. Our tradition is feed walkers. You hungry?' I nodded eagerly, the smell of the food making my stomach rumble.

'We're both vegetarian, though,' Gil said.

'No problem! No problem! Stay here. Drink, drink.'

We sat on the sofa sipping our chilled beers and watching the groups of people having shouted conversations above the music. Within a few minutes we had a paper plate in our laps full of grilled vegetables, hummus and salads. Before we'd finished the plate more food was added, brought to us by different family members. None of them spoke to us, they just seemed quite content knowing we were resting, drinking and eating – although it crossed my mind that maybe it was because they weren't comfortable speaking with me. I often felt like a burden not being able to speak Hebrew, forcing the people around me to speak English, even though most Israelis were fluent. I'd tried to learn Hebrew many times and had even done an intensive language course, but without much success. Hebrew, a Semitic language, has very few similarities to English. The alphabet is different, made of twenty-two characters which are written from right to left. There are new pronunciations to learn, from guttural sounds to rolling 'r's, and nouns are gendered, resulting in a language that my dyslexic brain just couldn't seem to grasp.

We sat for two hours, maybe more, until we realised we had to move on before the light ran away from us.

'Good luck!' they called after us as we walked away.

'That was amazing. I can't believe they just gave us all that beer and food,' I said to Gil, feeling the effects of the alcohol in my head and the food on my body. While the Israelis may be noisy and a little forceful by nature, no-one else can match them for generosity, which usually presents itself in the form of excessive feeding.

As darkness neared, a sun-kissed glow radiated from my soul. My stiff hair, salty from my sea swims, had turned noticeably blonder and there was sand in every crease of my body. As the beach thinned of people I reflected on what a great few days it had been until the last person of the day passed us. A man, wearing nothing but the tiniest pair of bright green Speedos I'd ever seen. His skin was dark and leathered from years spent in the sun and he was walking sideways, doing a strange sidestep like a crab scuttling on its back legs, arms up straight above his head, bent at the elbow. He turned his head and sniffed his armpit.

'*Shalom*,' hello, he nodded at me as he passed.

'*Shalom*,' I said back, grateful that there was enough distance between us that I wasn't going to find out what he had smelt.

Chapter 6

We were on our own again. Back on the familiar dusty, dry trail having finished our 'hikers' vacation' on the coastal stretch. The trail had taken us around the north of Tel Aviv, a city alive with car horns, street art and markets, past Reading Power Station. We walked by a marina packed with shiny yachts and signs of wealth before cutting through the famous Yarkon Park, full of runners and teams of people playing sport. Turning away from the park, we ducked through a graffiti-lined underpass and on to a path that led us away from the city.

Although I'd enjoyed the energy of Tel Aviv, and the luxury of sporadic falafel stands and convenience stores – meaning that more than once I had a giant chocolate bar for breakfast – I was ready to return to the remoteness of the trail, feeling a sense of unfinished business. *Is it possible I've even missed it?*

I was walking at a gentle pace, confident we had more than enough time to get where we needed to go, singing the lyrics to my favourite song.

'Under pressure that burns a building down, splits a family in two, puts people on streets…'

It was a song I'd sung as loudly as I could in a karaoke booth in London shortly before leaving for Israel, my friends, thankfully, as drunk as I was. *What were they all doing right now?* This question often popped into my head as I imagined them all on their commutes or sat at a desk or, if it was the weekend, having lie-ins and meeting up with friends. It made me wonder what I would be doing right this minute as well, as if I was living in a parallel universe and there was a Bex somewhere who hadn't decided to pack up her life and walk a trail. The answer to this was often quite easy to predict.

'… Turned away from it all like a blind man, sat on a fence but it don't work…'

I hummed the last of the song and then settled back into the silence around me. We were on a wide 4x4 dirt track which slowly meandered up through a wooded area, a mix of sharp brambles and dense trees surrounding us. I tuned into the sound of my hiking sticks hitting the ground and the scuff of my footsteps on the dirt. My muscles were stiff but not burning, I was hot and sweating but not to the point I felt sick.

The trail continued on a gentle upward incline and, when the path forked, we both made a point of double-checking the INT marker which definitely indicated to take the path leading right. The multiple times we'd missed a turning or misunderstood a pointer made us extra cautious on turnings like this. The worst of these times had been a week before when the trail had clashed with an existing route and the Red Book had guided us to switch to following the red markers for a short way before returning back to the INT. An hour in, we realised our mistake. We'd been following orange markers which, on the grubby rocks and walls, were easily mistaken for red. This had led us in completely the wrong direction and was a tear-filled error that added to an already difficult day.

At some point the trees opened up and in the distance we could make out the hazy silhouette of the city, high-rise blocks piercing the flat horizon. We both paused to catch our breath and I took a few sips from my hydration pack. It was too soon for a sit-down break so we continued on the path, back into the trees, slowly leading us up. The trail was heading towards Jerusalem, an ancient city that sits 745 metres above sea level, so we knew we had some climbing to do.

Three hours after setting off, we spotted a man perched on a boulder. He wore glasses, had a slight build with hunched shoulders, and was a similar age to us. There was no question, from the worn grey of his clothes and his rucksack, a foam roll mat attached to the outside, that he was a fellow long-distance hiker.

'Hey, are you doing the Israel National Trail?' I asked.

'Yes.'

'How long are you hiking for?' It was the standard first question every backpacker asks when they meet another.

'I'm doing the whole trail, what about you?' Ayal was the first hiker we had met who was planning to go the whole way and who wasn't preceding or post army service. He was genuine and void of the arrogance that I'd often seen in passing hikers, and I liked him instantly. We quickly backtracked over our hike to this point and worked out we'd started on exactly the same day. We'd bumped into exactly the same people, been fed by the same family on the beach, even camped just hundreds of metres from each other on some nights.

'How have we not met you until now?' Gil asked.

'I don't know, that's so strange.' Ayal offered us each a date from a plastic bag he was holding before stuffing them back in his bag and tightening the top with a drawstring. 'Can I join you hiking for a bit?'

For the rest of the day we got to know Ayal, enjoying the novelty of company. He told us about how he lives with a condition called haemophilia, a rare disorder in which blood doesn't clot normally because it lacks sufficient blood-clotting proteins. With no cure currently available, he relies on an expensive treatment that involves fortnightly injections for life to prevent bleeding. As these need to be refrigerated, Ayal was relying on travelling to and from the trail by bus when he needed to, or on his mum who would drive the medication to him.

'I have to get pretty creative when I travel. It's not always easy, like when I was in remote South America and there were always power cuts, but I manage.'

We continued on, sometimes in silence, sometimes chatting and sometimes I'd hang back allowing Gil and Ayal to speak in their native language. Reaching Latrun Forest, we joined what Gil said was the Burma Road. Gil read the description from the Red Book, which explained how the road had been constructed to bring food and ammunition to Jerusalem during the Arab-Israeli War.

We had agreed to aim that night for a picnic area in the forest which was a short walk from a gas station where we would be able to fill up with water. There were benches, a walled fire circle and lots of inviting flat ground to camp on.

We dropped our bags on the floor and set about putting up our tents. Because we'd been passing through the city it had been quite a few nights since we had last camped, and I was actually looking forward to it. For one night we'd stayed with Gil's old school friend, whose very fluffy cats shed so much hair that I was still plucking it from our clothes and sleeping bags. Another night we slept at the trendy Abraham Hostel and, the previous night, we were hosted by a Trail Angel, an experience neither of us wanted to repeat. The Trail Angel family were offering space for hikers to sleep in their martial arts studio and were conveniently placed just metres from the trail. Knowing it would be a while until we could next shower, we jumped at the chance, thinking it was also a great opportunity to meet new people. We texted the family, getting their number from the online

Trail Angel directory, asking if it was OK to stay, and they replied within minutes saying yes.

Looking at the map I calculated we had four kilometres to go before we reached their studio and, in the distance, I could just about make out a cluster of houses where I assumed we would be staying. I was settling into the last push of the day, knowing that it would take about an hour, when a jeep came tearing up the dirt track right towards us.

'Bex? Gil?' a man asked, sticking his head out of the window.

'Yes,' we said in unison.

'I'm Asaf, the Trail Angel, you stay with us tonight.' He got out of the jeep and we all shook hands.

'Are you Jewish?' he asked me.

'No, I'm not.'

'Do you speak Hebrew?'

'No. I understand a few words, but I do…'

'Why? You must learn Hebrew,' he said, interrupting me before I could finish. I just shrugged, feeling prickly from his insensitive interrogation. 'Get in and I'll drive you to the studio.'

'Thanks, although actually we prefer to walk if that's OK, as we don't want to miss any section of the trail. It won't take much longer to get to you, though,' I replied.

Asaf waved an arm as if brushing away what I had said. 'No, no, I'll drive you. Although first we drink coffee.'

He pulled out a coffee set from the back seat, a standard bit of kit it seems that every Israeli has on them at all times. He lit the stove and began the process of boiling water before mixing in strong aromatic Arabic coffee. Not only was I not a coffee drinker, but by late afternoon, down to the last of our water supplies, I was always so parched I wanted nothing more than to finish hiking and drink cool water until my stomach was nauseous from too much liquid.

There's lots of debate among Israelis as to the 'correct' way of making coffee but Asaf used a similar technique to the one I'd seen Gil use many times before. He brought the small pot of coffee up to boiling, making sure not to stir the powder once it had been added to the water, then removed it from the heat. He then returned it to the flame until it stared boiling once more, and removed it quickly. He repeated this multiple times, added sugar, stirred and then served into shot-size ceramic cups to drink.

I could see Gil also didn't want to drink coffee but we drank it out of politeness. As I sipped the thick, bitter liquid, I hoped that at least now he would be less pushy about driving us to his place.

'You want another one?' he asked me.

'No thank you, although that was really nice.' He took the cup from my hand and filled it with coffee anyway. I waited until he wasn't looking, then threw the hot liquid into the shrubbery by the side of the road.

'Come on, *yalla*, *yalla*,' Asaf said, packing away the coffee kit and throwing it haphazardly into the back seat before indicating we should follow.

'We do really want to walk there,' Gil tried again. 'We don't want to miss any section of the trail.'

'Who cares? No-one will know. Get in.' Asaf, leaving the passenger door open, climbed into the driver's seat before starting the engine. Gil looked at me helplessly with a small shrug. Once upon a time he would have argued more firmly, but six years living in London and British politeness had rubbed off on him. Neither of us could refuse someone who was being kind enough to host us, it just seemed too rude.

'We'll just have to walk back to this spot tomorrow morning,' I whispered to Gil as we climbed into the jeep, making a note of an unusual-looking tree that we could use as a marker. It would be frustrating walking here just to turn around and walk back, but I couldn't see another way. We'd covered hundreds of kilometres to reach this point, not missing a single section of the trail. It might seem pedantic to some but there was no way we were skipping even a hundred metres now. It felt like cheating. Each hiker had their own way of doing things, their own self-inflicted rules, and this was ours. We'd set ourselves a goal to walk the trail and I got satisfaction from knowing we were experiencing every marker en route on foot, without exception.

Asaf drove us back to his martial arts studio. I was annoyed with myself for not standing my ground but instead chose to focus on the fact that we could shower and eat soon and, thanks to their generosity, we wouldn't have to put up a tent, having, what I hoped, would be a good, uninterrupted night's sleep.

Arriving at the studio we met Asaf's wife and one of their grown-up children, Ben. Nothing highlights your own hiking filth more than standing next to squeaky-clean, civilised people who have not spent the day sweating their way through a sand pit. The urge to shower, change clothes and eat was almost animalistic, but first we needed to do the mandatory introductions. The family showed us around, and then started to tell us about all the hikers they had hosted. They brought out a guest book and took us through it page by page, highlighting all the praise they'd been given.

'We've hosted more hikers than anyone else,' Asaf said, as if it were some sort of competition. Then they started to talk about holidays they'd been on; the photo books came out for that.

We nodded and smiled, listening to what felt like a day-by-day breakdown of every place they had been to over the past ten years. Next, the attention turned to Ben, who was a keen athlete. When we were directed to the study so they could show us his medals and videos of him competing, I saw my opportunity and quickly slipped away to the shower.

I could have stayed locked in that bathroom all night but I thought about Gil all on his own keeping up the pretence of being interested and at least now that I was clean and in fresh clothes, I was more comfortable. I swapped with Gil and, just as I thought surely this couldn't get any worse, the wedding video came out. How I longed to be sat dirty in our tent hidden behind some bush right now. Heck, I'd even prefer to have to climb Mount Tabor again than to be stuck in this situation. Three hours of showing off was really starting to test me.

Asaf looked at his watch and jumped up. 'We are meeting someone. We need to go for a bit.'

'OK,' I said, trying not to look too pleased about this news.

'We'll come back in about an hour, though.'

We waved them off from the porch and, as soon as they were out of sight, both sat down on the top step.

'Bloody hell,' Gil said, 'I thought it was never going to end.'

As he set about cooking spaghetti for dinner on the porch – not wanting to light the stove inside in case we accidentally caused any damage – I laid out the roll mats and sleeping bags in the middle of the studio where they'd instructed us to sleep. Asaf's wife had said it was OK to use the equipment so I grabbed one of the foam rollers from the corner and attempted to stretch out my legs. Twisting forward so the weight of my body was on my thigh, I rolled back and forth. Putting pressure on the knots in my muscles was excruciating and I lasted about ten seconds before deciding the pain wasn't worth it and I'd stick to having stiff legs instead.

It was much later than we would normally eat and, now it was dark, we were both feeling the cold. Gil brought the pan of spaghetti inside and we sat up in our sleeping bags, taking it in turns to have a mouthful each until the pan was empty and every bit of sauce scraped clean. When we heard a vehicle pulling up outside Gil leaped up like he was being shot at, sprinted across the room and switched the lights off.

'Lie down, lie down! Don't move,' he yelled at me, now trying to get back into his sleeping bag, his frantic leg kicks causing the bag to tangle up.

'Quick!' I hissed as the front door opened. We both flopped down and lay still. I waited a moment and then half-opened my eyes. Reflected in the studio mirror I could make out three people, their hands pressed up against the window that separated the studio from the reception area. I stayed very still, barely daring to breathe. They stood peering in for so long that, for a moment, I was worried they were going to come in and 'wake' us, but thankfully they turned around and left.

I felt guilty that we'd lied our way out of spending more time with them, but I was exhausted. We didn't bother turning the lights back on. It was 8.40pm, an acceptable hikers' bedtime.

A few hours later I was disturbed by the sound of something moving around nearby. I sat up, the hairs standing up on the back of my neck as my imagination started to conjure up explanations for what could be causing it. I turned on my head torch and waved the beam around the room but couldn't see anything out of place.

The noise started up again and this time I could make out the distinct sound of claws scuttling back and forth on a hard surface. There was clearly an animal living in the roof overhead.

'Rats,' Gil mumbled. I turned off my light and settled back down into my sleeping bag.

'I feel strange sleeping here. Like I've broken into a gym. And I keep thinking they're going to come back.'

'Yeah, me too. Let's mostly camp from now on.'

'Agreed.'

* * * *

Gil and Ayal were collecting kindling and wood from around the picnic area to make a fire. I left them to it, everyone's water bottles balanced in my arms, making my way to the gas station which the map told me was a short walk away. While I was there I asked the shop assistant if I could charge our battery pack for twenty minutes to give it a boost. He took it from me and plugged it in behind the tills and I went outside to sit on the kerb while I waited. I watched the cars driving back and forth on the busy road, fascinated by the speed of everyone rushing about going to and from places. The car park was empty except for two men who climbed out of an old white car that looked like it should have been scrapped years ago. From the boot, they took out pizza takeaway boxes which they opened out flat. They laid them on the floor and began praying, using the boxes as a prayer mat.

By the time I had returned to camp, weighed down with water, the fire was lit and I took my spot by the warm glow. A familiar sound interrupted our conversation and an army helicopter flew right overhead, the bass cutting through my ribcage. Although it must have been incredibly close, we couldn't see it.

'They're flying blind,' Ayal said. 'They're practising moving around at night with no lights.'

Then came the sound of crunching metal, creeping slowly towards us from the darkness. As it got near, Ayal shone his torch in the direction of the sound, illuminating a large tank moving its way along the dirt track just metres from us. Then came the soldiers running behind, faces smeared with camouflage, large rucksacks on their backs, rifles in hand. Ayal took great pleasure in shining his torch on them while they pretended that we weren't there.

My hope that they were just passing through was short-lived. Throughout the night, we were woken multiple times by the helicopter deafening us as it flew around above our heads, while various vehicles moved back and forth until, at about one in the morning, it all fell silent and we were finally able to sleep.

I woke the next morning, my mood frostier than normal. I counted to five in my head, accepting the inevitable, then sat up to get changed into my hiking clothes, keeping my limbs in the warmth of the sleeping bag as long as possible, putting things on one at a time. They were still a bit damp from the day before.

I then headed off into the trees to a secluded spot to have a wee and brush my teeth, before packing down the inside of the tent while Gil started to pull out the tent pegs and roll up the guy ropes. We folded down the tent together, packed our individual bags, each item now with a permanent home, threw on our packs and were ready to go.

It was the same routine we followed every morning, each of us now knowing what we needed to do without having to say anything, and it rarely took us more than twenty minutes. We both liked it this way. I found that starting to hike was like pulling off a plaster: better to do it quickly and not hang about. The slow mornings were the hardest and, the longer we held off from starting, the more the voices of doubt started up in my head. Walking with Ayal meant accepting a different pace but I had little patience, thanks mostly to being caught in the middle of an exercise war zone the night before.

'I'll walk alone for a bit and see you both at the first viewpoint,' I said, pointing at Mishlat 21 on the map, a military post at the peak of Mount Orna, about an hour's walk from where we were. I headed off, happy to have a bit of space to shake off my morning grouchiness.

I marvelled at the view from Mishlat 21, the sunrise giving the colours of the surrounding trees and hills a soft quality. Six million trees had been planted below, near the Bnei Brit Memorial Cave, a tree for every Holocaust victim, each one representing a person of ambition, hopes and dreams. It was a reminder to me that, even without all the complications of the current conflict, this was also a country built on unimaginable trauma. A trauma that was still a living memory in most families, including Gil's: his grandmother carried with her a childhood of displacement and concentration camps, and time spent in a British refugee camp in Cyprus following World War II. It was rarely spoken about but there was no doubt that the horrors of the past were ingrained in all of Gil's family and, I imagine, most Jewish people living across the world.

Checking my watch, I calculated that I maybe had about twenty minutes before Gil and Ayal caught up with me. It was a good opportunity to fix a niggle that I was feeling in my right foot. I reached for the tub of Vaseline that I kept conveniently in the top of my pack, and pulled my sock down halfway, scooping a large chunk of the ointment and rubbing it on to my ankle where the skin was looking red. I'd been strict with my own laziness since the day we'd run out of water, experiencing first-hand how it can quickly escalate to create a bigger problem. So now, any time I noticed a spot getting sore on my foot I immediately applied Vaseline, a tip that had never yet failed to prevent a blister developing.

Later that day we parted ways with Ayal, who decided to catch a bus into Jerusalem to take a rest day.

'I really hope we see you again on the trail,' he said to us.

'Yeah, me too,' I said, genuinely. I'd really enjoyed his company. We exchanged numbers, promising to try our best to meet again before the end.

The trail continued upwards, hugging the outskirts of Jerusalem and taking us higher still on to the top of a hill where we decided to camp near a tiny spring. The slow, persistent climb had taken its toll on my legs so I placed them in the icy water until the blood was pounding in my calves and the skin was tingling on my feet. Taking my legs out, I lay in the tent, my feet raised on my bag, and enjoyed the sensation of them being numb.

From where we were, I could make out the outskirts of Jerusalem to the right, a scattering of the city's signature light stone-bricked houses. To the left was dense forest as far as I could see and, nestled in there somewhere, a rave, the sound of the music reaching us on the wind once in a while. When we left the next morning at 5am, the rave was still going.

As I was walking away from the camp, my heart skipped when the beam of my light caught two shining eyes peering at us from just beyond the bushes. I stared back, the floating, unblinking eyes boring through me before disappearing. A few moments later, a howling began, building to a crescendo as the pack of jackals all joined in the call. It surrounded us on all sides and sent shivers down my spine. As quickly as it had started, it was over, the pack falling into a unanimous and perfectly timed silence, but I still felt their presence and eyes on me as I walked away.

As I plodded along the path, keeping time with the distant sound of thumping bass, I thought about all the people at the rave who had been up all night. It could have been us partying, out for a night in London. Clean and dressed up, knocking back shots with friends and stumbling around in the early hours in search of a bag of chips. My priority always to drink as much as I could, dance until I was exhausted and time the last drink well enough so I didn't have too unbearable a hangover the next day. Now our priorities were food, sleep and covering distance on foot. There were things that I missed a lot about the life I had left behind, but the longing didn't run deeper than for superficial luxuries like a mattress and a fridge full of food.

The music eventually stopped around 6am, just as we were reaching the bottom of the hill. As the ravers were heading home, we were heading out to hike thirty kilometres. Different worlds, just a stone's throw apart.

Chapter 7

I was taken aback by the sudden open space that lay ahead of me. One minute I'd been hiking through vineyards, sneakily grabbing handfuls of red grapes, the next I had turned into what felt like an infinite void. It looked like a big machine had come along and dragged away everything in its path, leaving nothing but wide-open space. It was a taster of the challenge that lay ahead, the desert that was nearing us as we continued south. In four days' time, we would reach Arad and, from that point, we would be properly in the Negev.

The physical support from family had come to an end and the day before we'd said goodbye to Mira and Amir. They'd met us for the last time to bring us cooked meals and company. We wouldn't see them again until after we had finished the trek, the distance now too far from their home for them to travel. Although we'd only met them a handful of times, there had been great comfort in seeing them and their visits had always provided something to look forward to, something to work towards.

I popped a grape in my mouth, its juice so sweet it caused my jaw to ache, and then set off into the space ahead. My mind was firmly focused on the rest day we planned to take in Arad.

The next fifteen kilometres were flat and almost featureless. The monotony of the landscape meant that my sense of movement and understanding of distance covered was lost. It felt like I wasn't making any progress, even though my legs were pounding. It led me to speed up, leaving Gil behind at his own pace, but still the horizon continued to stretch on forever, never quite within reach.

Eventually, a small cluster of eucalyptus trees came into view and, when I reached their welcoming shade, I sat down and waited for Gil. I could have happily eaten lunch but, as it was only 10am, I settled on a few dried apricots instead.

'Man, you're walking fast,' Gil said, joining me in the shade.

'I felt good! You shouldn't try to keep up pace with me, though, especially with your foot.'

'It's fine. My foot is feeling a lot better today.' Gil's right foot had been swelling and causing him pain for the last few days. He'd called a doctor who had advised him to massage, elevate and wrap the foot in cabbage leaves overnight. The trail had a shortage of cabbages so Gil had to make do with my foot massages and resting it on his bag whenever we took a break.

Our plan had been to cover twenty-three kilometres, but as we reached our intended camping spot before midday we decided to continue for another hour, noticing a small wooded area on the map that could make a good alternative. Cutting through the trees, I spotted the perfect place, a mostly flat circle hidden by bushes. It was the earliest we'd finished yet and, once the tent was up, just the netting part without the waterproof outer, we still had four hours before it got dark.

'I'm going to have a nap,' Gil declared, climbing on top of his roll mat and zipping up the door so the flies wouldn't bother him.

'OK, enjoy.' I stood for a moment and pondered what to do myself. I've often envied Gil's ease with sleeping and his ability to lie down, any time of day, and be snoozing with no more than a moment's notice. My relationship with sleep had definitely changed on the trail as I'd experienced exhaustion like never before. I'd been going to bed earlier and sleeping longer, and my insomnia, which had bothered me for years in London, rarely paid a visit anymore. I wasn't ready for sleep, though, after such an easy day hiking, the easiest yet. In fact, I was feeling uncharacteristically energised. I'd packed a small Kindle with me, not able to bear being away from books for such a long time, but instead of reading I opted for the one thing I looked forward to each evening once the need for food and dry clothes had been dealt with: catching up with my blog.

* * * *

At some point during the process of getting ready for the hike, I had decided to launch a blog. The hike gave me a topic that, for the first time in my life, justified having an online journal and a reason to put my words out publicly. It's a sad fact that I felt like I needed permission to do something that I'd always wanted to do. Ever since I was little, I had dreamt of being a writer but the older I got, the less I believed in my work. It was something that no doubt stemmed from my inability to spell or get my words down coherently due to having undiagnosed dyslexia for most of my early years. It was something that defined my schooling, my teachers reinforcing the idea that I should be ashamed of my writing.

'How do you expect to be a writer one day if you can't even do basic spelling? Your spelling level is barely above a seven-year-old's. It's not good enough,' my English teacher had told my teenage self after class one day when I'd failed yet another spelling test. She made me write the misspelt words out a hundred times each.

Never quite feeling understood by my teachers stopped me from reaching my full potential in most subjects. Alongside this,

I was chubby, a product of my unhappy comfort eating, and far too clumsy to be good at sport, so I found myself loitering in the creative departments which seemed to be there to scoop up the misfits who didn't fit in anywhere else. By the time I left school, I didn't need my teachers or grades to tell me my work wasn't good enough because it was a narrative I was firmly telling myself.

With so many changes happening in my life and the petrifying decision to do the hike already made, it didn't feel like much to throw another scary step into the mix. It took me months to design and learn how to create a blog, and then even longer to actually write and finally publish my first post. I'd redrafted it a dozen times. Of course, only a handful of friends and family would read it but I still wanted it to be perfect.

Finding a cosy space next to a tree, I laid down my fleece to make the ground a bit more comfortable to sit on. I opened the portable solar panel I'd been carrying and placed it in the sun before plugging it into the phone to give it some charge while I wrote. As soon as the screen was on, my thumbs began typing at a frantic speed, capturing my thoughts unfiltered and with absolute honesty. I was enjoying having my own little space in the world to express all the experiences I'd had that day. Writing it in my own way and without anyone breathing down my neck telling me to do otherwise.

There was no room for perfection in my writing on the hike. The screen was small and the time I could spend writing short because the battery needed to be kept fully charged in case of an emergency. Once I'd finished the post, I saved it on the phone ready to publish as soon as we found signal.

My writing was full of spelling and grammatical errors and far from groundbreaking literature, but it didn't seem to matter. Very gradually, my readership began to increase, tiny drops of water in a cup, the kind of trickle that you don't notice until the cup is surprisingly full. People who I didn't know were following my journal and leaving me messages saying how much they enjoyed reading it and how inspiring they found my words. I'd had a few offers of sponsorship, including from Abraham Hostel, who had offered us a free night's stay in exchange for me writing about it in a blog post. Then something had happened a couple of days before that I still couldn't quite believe. We'd just come down a hill and were sitting outside a rural gas station to catch our breath before going inside to pick up some snacks and refill our water.

A young man was making a beeline for me, leaving a small group who were sat around a picnic table.

'Do you have a blog?' he asked. For a dusty hiker he looked impressively stylish, with a full beard, long hair tied back, an Afghan scarf around his neck and a large-lensed camera casually hanging from one hand.

'Um, I do.'

'Bex, right?'

'Yeah.' My eyebrows shot up.

'I thought I recognised you. I read some of your blogs; they're really great.' I was so taken aback I didn't know what to say. 'I did some searching before starting the hike and that's how I found your site and your kit list.'

'Really?' I said, hoping he wasn't about to tell me how much gear he had been missing.

'It was actually really helpful.'

'Wow! Thank you!'

'Thank *you*. I'm Gadi.'

I took his outstretched hand and he gave me a light squeeze. I asked about his huge camera, amazed that someone could carry all that extra weight.

'I'm a photography student, so wanted to capture some of my trip on the INT. You want to see some of my pictures?' Gadi cupped his hand around the screen and we both leant closer so we could see the photos as he flicked through. They were incredible. Showing so many details I never would have noticed and capturing the faces of people he passed along the way.

'Keep writing,' Gadi shouted to me as we said our goodbyes and walked away.

'I will. Keep taking pictures,' I called back. When we were out of earshot Gil turned to me.

'Don't say anything,' I said, unsuccessfully trying to hide a smile.

'Sure,' he held up his hands. 'Just don't let the fame go to your head.'

For the rest of the day I carried with me a feeling I hadn't experienced for a long time. I was proud.

* * * *

I practically bounded out of bed knowing that the next day we would be reaching Arad. The longing for a cold meal and to rinse the dirt away from my body nagged at me like an itch I couldn't reach. While Gil went for one final wee before we headed off, I looked at the map, setting my expectations for the day. Today it was my turn to navigate. There would be a fair bit of climbing to do, nothing major, but lots of ups and downs. Gil and I had started to use the phrase 'what goes down must come up', knowing that any downhill on the trail was short-lived. Hiking on the trail reminded me of the time I had a job stacking shelves as a teenager. I'd spend hours filling the shelves carefully with tins and packets until they were full, rows of neat lines with not a gap to be seen, always a bit obsessive about having the labels facing out at the same angle, only to return for my next shift and find the shelves empty again. It was a task that never had the satisfaction of completion.

When Gil returned, we did our usual sweep of the area, making sure we'd left nothing behind and that there was no trace that we'd been there at all. After briefly debating whether to find a spot in the woods, we'd camped in another picnic area; the prospect of a bench to eat dinner on had won the argument. There was a small farming town nearby called Kibbutz Dvira but, as we hadn't seen anyone for days, I was sure we wouldn't be disturbed. But of course, as with so many of our nights on the trail, this was not the case. Shortly after midnight our tent was flooded with a bright light that had us both sitting up startled from sleep and blinking in the glare. Gil unzipped the tent door and I could make out a car, the headlamps on us, and a man stood in front of it wearing a fabric poncho and a large-brimmed hat. He raised both his arms, palms facing us.

'I do not wish to alarm you, I saw you earlier so don't be nervous, we won't disturb you. I've come here with friends and we won't cause problems. I wish you the best for the journey.' He brought his palms together and bowed his head slightly.

'Uh, sure,' Gil said, blinking from the light. The man returned to his car and drove it a few metres away to the bench furthest from us. A reggae song started blaring from the car as people piled out. I groaned, flopping back down on to my roll mat. Thankfully, they only played that one song before settling down quietly to smoke weed. It was the first time I'd seen Israeli Jews and Israeli Arabs socialising together. If the strange guy hadn't woken us up with the lights and with that one song, we wouldn't have even known they were there.

'What's this line on the map?' I asked Gil when he returned from his wee. 'I can't work it out.'

I was pointing to a thick, grey, winding dotted line. There was nothing marked to say what it was.

'That's the border with the West Bank.' Looking back at the map I saw the trail would be following the line for most of the day.

The sun started to rise as we ascended the first major hill in Lahav North Nature Reserve but grey clouds and thick fog prevented any sunlight from reaching us. We'd planned to take a break at the top, but a damp cloud descended on us along with strong winds which kept our legs moving. As the light revealed the reserve around us a chill shuddered through me, and not just from the cold. The area had been victim to wildfires, the entire landscape burnt to a black crisp. Occasionally we'd see a glimmer of life, a small green sprout of a weed or a beetle scuttling across a rock, but mostly there was nothing but black and charred bush remains. The eeriness was made worse by the fog, which was now increasing in density.

'Can you see the trail?' Gil called back from a few metres in front, head ducked into the wind. The path underfoot had lost any definition. I backtracked a bit looking for a marker while Gil went on ahead. With no landmarks, path or trail markers it was hard to know what direction to take but we kept pushing forward. As we came down the final hill out of the reserve, the fog lifted in a matter of minutes, instantly warming our skin. It turned out that we'd been walking a few hundred metres south of the trail so we dropped down to get back on the correct path.

Ahead of us, I saw for the first time the huge wire fence cutting a line separating Israel and the West Bank. The top was wound with menacing-looking barbed wire and large CCTV cameras. We found ourselves walking within metres of it at one point. On the other side was a large barren space with some boys kicking a football around, and beyond that houses and short blocks of flats. At one point I could see the border with the West Bank in the distance, a queue of cars on both sides looking to pass the barriers.

As the last of the afternoon light started to creep away, we found ourselves on the series of ups and downs that I had been anticipating. It had been an uneventful afternoon, although I had found time to call my mum – there had been a stretch with signal and I knew we would be in Arad the next day and could afford to use up some of the phone's battery life.

'How is it going?' my mum asked.

'Yeah, good. It's hard. And hot.' I wasn't really sure what else to say.

'I'm enjoying reading your blogs. You talk about food a lot.'

I laughed. 'Yeah, I'm hungry. Pretty much all the time.'

My mum filled me in on her work and on my nephew who had made an appearance just days before our departure and had 'grown so much' and was 'smiling loads'. I thought that I should tell her more about our hike but there was, in equal parts, too much to say and nothing at all. It was all so significant while also being nothing more than a monotony of simple day-to-day tasks, so I settled instead on simply listening to her talk about everything that was happening at home.

The wind had really started to pick up, so much so that as we reached the top of another hill I had to brace my body and fight against its force, worried it would topple me over.

'I hope we can find somewhere to sleep,' Gil shouted above the roar.

'I know – I'm not sure our tent will cope with this.'

'Do you think we can make it to the picnic area?'

I shook my head. 'The wind has been slowing us down too much. Let's keep going, though, and see if we can find somewhere sheltered.'

Two more hills later and a small cluster of trees, the start of Meitar woods, provided just what we needed. Although we usually only put up the inner part of the tent, we decided to also throw on the outer nylon layer, its dark green hiding us from anyone who might pass by. We weren't sure if we were allowed to camp here, especially with the border just a few hundred metres away.

I sat by the tent watching Gil, who was crouched over the stove preparing dinner, improvising making garlic bread by mixing together flour, water, salt and garlic cloves which he moulded into flat circles before cooking lightly on both sides. We both froze when we heard a vehicle approaching. An open military truck passed by on the trail we'd just been on, bouncing over the bumpy road. Four soldiers sat on top and, despite it passing just a few steps from us, none of them spotted us or the tent. We were invisible to anyone not paying attention.

Within seconds I felt a drop of water on my face, then another. We rushed about collecting our bits and throwing them into the tent as the rain started to build up to a gentle but consistent downpour.

'Good job we put up the outer,' Gil said.

'What are the chances? Maybe we should have kept our waterproofs?' I said, as an afterthought. We'd left them behind in Zichron Ya'akov as we hadn't used them at all in the first weeks.

'It won't last long, you'll see.'

Gil was right. Within an hour, the rain had eased, leaving behind a dramatic skyline of grey clouds and a pink sunset.

It was the first and only time it rained during our time on the trail.

* * * *

One minute we were walking in nothingness and the next we stepped on to a road to find ourselves in civilisation. We had reached Arad, a city on the border of the Negev, with a population of 26,000. I couldn't quite get my head around the stark contrast: desert if I looked behind me and built-up city if I looked ahead. Before taking another step I instinctively tensed, my heart lurching as I spotted something moving out of the corner of my eye. A long yellow snake crossed our path as it escaped from the front garden of one of the nearby houses. It slithered sideways, its body in a wave formation, and became difficult to see once it reached the desert floor, its colouring camouflaging it perfectly.

It was a relief to reach the city but the underlying nerves I had been carrying were suddenly hard to ignore. Arad meant a rest stop, but it was also the start of the desert stretch of the trail. Everything from now on would be different. Gone would be the villages, towns, farms and forests and all that lay ahead would be thirteen thousand square kilometres of Negev desert and a path that snaked right down its middle. The task of crossing it had been pushed to the back of my mind since the day we committed to doing the trail. It was the most daunting part of the hike, a place where many have lost their lives. Some from flash flooding, a strange phenomenon caused by sudden heavy downpours running off the dry ground, causing dangerous amounts of water to filter into the dry riverbeds and valleys, known as wadis, at incredible force and speed. Any hiker walking in a riverbed when a flash flood hit would have just minutes to get to safety. Others had lost their lives due to lack of water and the heat in an environment that saw the country's hottest temperatures by day but bitterly cold nights. The terrain also became a lot more challenging underfoot, with tougher and more frequent climbs, more scrabbling and a higher risk of getting lost, falling and injury.

No longer able to rely on sporadic farms, supermarkets, gas stations or picnic areas for water and food, we'd had to plan this section meticulously to ensure we could continue safely. We'd need to carry much more food with us for each section and for water would now be relying on a system known as water caching. We'd spoken with a man named Yanir who was well known among hikers in Israel for providing this service, hiding water on the trail in predesignated areas. Yanir had driven his jeep into the desert ahead of us to leave our water supply under rocks, behind bushes or tucked into alcoves, and had sent us a video of each of the hiding spots which we'd saved on our phone ready for when we'd need them.

First, though, we had a rest day and I was determined to make the most of it. Food, a shower and sleep were in touching distance at the hostel we'd booked to stay at for the next two nights. With our supply packs empty, though, our priority was to stop at a supermarket on the way.

'You stay with the bags and I'll get the food,' I said, dropping my rucksack on the floor by the automatic doors.

'Are you sure you don't want me to help? It's a big shop.'

'I've got this one.'

As Gil had been taking the lead with the shopping up to now I felt it was my turn to give him a break. I hate shopping at the best of times, but doing it in Israel brings a whole different level of stress.

Everything is in Hebrew, the food and brands unfamiliar, and the supermarket shelves claustrophobic and disorganised.

'Is there anything you want me to get you?'

'Bamba,' Gil replied, asking for an Israeli brand of peanut-flavoured puffed crisps.

I entered the supermarket, ignoring the complaints from my empty stomach that only seemed to get louder at the sight of all the food, and gripping our carefully planned shopping list scribbled on the back of an old receipt. This was an especially important shop as the next opportunity to resupply wouldn't be for another six days, our longest stretch yet. Thinking of the full week of isolation without the reassurance of shops or modern-day conveniences nearby made my stomach knot. I set off with my trolley, taking one aisle at a time, collecting nuts, dates, tahini, couscous, while also throwing in anything that took my fancy that we could eat during our rest day: pastries, salad, crisps, potatoes, sugary treats. I ticked off the list as I went, filling the trolley, until I had just one item left to get – pumpkin seeds. I couldn't see them anywhere. Leaving the trolley at one end of the aisle, to make it easier to search, I started scanning the shelves trying to find them. At last, I located the seeds and made my way back to the trolley. Only it wasn't there. I paced up and down but couldn't see it anywhere.

'Excuse me, I had a trolley full of shopping but I can't find it,' I asked a shop assistant by the tills, a man with long hair and thick-rimmed glasses.

'I don't know where it is,' he shrugged.

'Well... obviously it's been moved.'

An elderly lady leaned over me and asked the assistant something in Hebrew. He instantly replied and started to walk away.

'Excuse me, I asked for your help first,' I said, feeling a bit petty but also not wanting him just to ignore me.

'What do you want me to do?'

'I don't know. Help me find it. Probably someone who works in the shop moved it.'

He pushed his glasses up the bridge of his nose and the old lady, who had been glaring at me the whole time, shuffled off.

'Fine. Wait here.'

I waited by the vegetable aisle as instructed. Then waited some more, until I started to think that maybe he had just abandoned me. Eventually, though, he returned, wheeling an empty trolley which he parked in front of me.

'I don't want an empty trolley! I want the trolley with my shopping in.'

'I said, I don't know where it is.'

'I put in a five-shekel coin to unlock my trolley. I want my five shekels!' I could hear my voice getting a little shrill.

'Well… this is the only trolley I could find.' He shrugged again.

I could feel my eyes welling and a lump forming at the back of my throat. I stormed out of the supermarket to Gil who was sitting on his bag, leaning against the wall. He looked up at my tears with bewilderment as I explained to him what had happened.

'Stay with the bags. I'll sort this,' he said firmly, standing up.

Ten minutes later Gil returned wheeling a shopping trolley full of food now in paper bags.

I stayed crouched on the floor like a weary child incapable of controlling their emotions or of carrying out a simple task. Without a word, Gil handed me a carton of orange juice and tore open a pitta bread which he filled with a large spoonful of chocolate spread. I took it reluctantly. If I wasn't already feeling like a child for the way I'd dealt with the situation, I sure felt like one now.

'Maybe we'll just stick to me doing the shopping,' he said, tucking into the rest of the pitta.

* * * *

Usually on rest days I wanted to sit or lie down, moving as little as possible for as long as possible, but I woke the next day in Arad feeling energised and wanting to be like all the other visitors in the area, a proper tourist. Staying in a hostel, we had the luxury of meeting an eclectic mix of people who were visiting from all over the world, from a French lady who was spending six weeks bathing in the nearby Dead Sea in the hope it would cure her skin condition to a couple from America who were here as part of a religious tour. On our first evening, we sat around a fire in the garden with them and, once they'd found out the reason for us being in the country, were littered with questions.

'How far have you walked?' Piero, a middle-aged Italian man with tight curly hair, asked us.

'About five hundred kilometres so far,' I said, and everybody gasped in amazement.

It was strange being the centre of attention and being awash with praise. Until now, most of the people we had met were hikers, most of them fitter, stronger and walking faster than us, so to them we were nothing special. But here, sat around the fire with new acquaintances from all over the globe, what we were doing was something to be marvelled at.

Since Zichron Ya'akov I hadn't given much thought to the distance we had travelled, but saying 'five hundred kilometres' out loud felt almost surreal. We were halfway. Watching the flames flicker in the fire, I wondered how many people in the world would ever walk such a distance and how, for much of the walk, I had believed I would never be one of them. I was not the only one who hadn't thought we could do it. My mind took me back to the first day on the trail, when we'd stopped by a cemetery for a break. Two gardeners were trimming the hedges into perfect rectangles.

'How far are you planning to go?' one of them asked us. Gil replied that we were intending to walk more than a thousand kilometres, all the way to Eilat. They looked at each other and both burst out laughing.

'Good luck with that,' one of them mocked, before turning back to trim the hedge. Their laughs rang in my ears for days.

One of the travellers who joined us around the fire was Ray, a teenage guy from Germany. Ray was of the Baha'i faith, a religion I'd never heard of. It was a new religion, he explained, and told us how he believed in the essential worth of all religions and in the unity of all people. How, for a long time, it was one of the fastest-growing religions in the world; that he didn't drink and that his faith forbids sex before marriage. Ray was spending a year in Israel volunteering in the city of Haifa at one of the religion's most sacred places, the Baha'i Gardens. The following day he was planning to visit the Dead Sea, the reason why most visitors passed through Arad, and invited us to join him.

The drive there was spectacular. The road meandered down through the mountains, roadside markers announcing how far below sea level we were, until we reached 430.5 metres – the world's lowest elevation on land – and the lake itself. The Dead Sea is truly impressive: long, silvery blue and encompassed by tall rugged mountains, Israel on one side and on the other Jordan. It was impossible to ignore, however, the south section of the lake, which has been industrialised, mined for its minerals and salts.

As soon as we arrived at the shore, we stripped off our clothes and joined the dozens of tourists, most of whom were of the OAP category, in the water. Once up to knee height I fell backwards, experiencing the strange sensation of my body popping up to the surface as if being held by hands from below. Because of the Dead Sea's high salt content, anyone who swims in it floats.

It took longer than we'd hoped to get back to our hostel. Ray had wanted to stay on to do a short hike to a nearby spring, so we'd tried, unsuccessfully, to hitchhike back to the city. Eventually, we admitted defeat and waited for the slow bus. Once we were dropped at the terminal, it took us another thirty minutes to walk to our accommodation.

'You're very quiet,' Gil said to me as I packed my bag ready for the next day, feeling all the day's relaxation slip away.

'Oh, it's nothing. I'm just not looking forward to tomorrow.'

'Me either. It's always hard starting after a rest day.'

'I'm also dreading the fact it gets harder. I'm not sure I'm ready for all the climbing and the heat.'

'Don't think about the whole desert crossing. Just focus on Mount Karbolet, the next milestone.'

According to the Red Book, Mount Karbolet was the most strenuous day on the entire INT, although it also promised to be the most beautiful. It was a five-day walk from where we were and a day we were both nervously anticipating. We'd had many hard days on the trail, but imagining anything tougher than those, so tough that even an expert hiker would say so in his guide, filled me with dread.

'What do you always tell me?' Gil continued. 'Look how far we've come, not at what's ahead.'

'I'm just quoting nonsense to make me sound wiser than I am,' I replied, making Gil laugh. 'Maybe we'll just stay in this hostel for a month instead. We could spend our days reading, chatting round fires and swimming in the Dead Sea.' I let myself daydream on that thought for a moment.

'Why would you want to do that when we could be suffering and sweating in the desert?'

Why indeed? We could have chosen to stay in hostels, gone to South America or Asia, like so many other travellers, to sit on beaches in the day and drink from buckets through plastic straws in the evening. I picked up my bag to test the weight, grunting with the effort. With six days' worth of food supplies and five litres of water it felt like I'd filled it with bricks.

'You'll be fine. You know how it is. Once you get going it's never as bad as you think.'

Gil turned me around so my back was against his legs where he sat on the bunk bed and began giving me a gentle shoulder massage. I knew he was right but it did little to shift the nerves. Tomorrow felt like the start of a new hike, the point where we began 'proper' hiking. The room for error lessened. Belief in my own abilities was wavering. The Negev would be the real test.

Chapter 8

I went to jump but then instantly tensed, changing my mind and gripping on to the rock with both hands so I wouldn't slip.

'It's not so far. Just remember to bend your knees when you land,' Gil said.

'Not helpful,' I replied.

It looked like we were walking in a giant tub of ice cream. We were in Nahal Kanfan, where the light-coloured rocks around us had a unique shape: large, meandering scoops cut through the land in swirling corridors caused by years of erosion from flooding. I'd never seen a landscape like it and had excitedly taken dozens of pictures for the first hour as we scrambled our way through the corridors. I was soon learning, though, that, although our surroundings were beautiful, they were really hard to navigate. The climb down was becoming steeper and the smooth rock provided little in the way of nooks or handles to aid climbing.

This particular drop was about a metre and a half long, down a narrow, funnel-shaped space. My moment of hesitation made me doubt my ability to make the jump, my mind now overthinking it, worried that I might land awkwardly and do myself an injury.

'I'll throw my pack down first,' I said, backing up and unclipping my bag, which I threw down the funnel. Gil moved it out of the way and, without the heavy weight on my back, I swiftly jumped down. Looking back, the distance looked disappointingly small from below.

'The place we crossed back there was called Gibson Pass,' Gil said, his face now in the Red Book. 'It's named after a hiker who had a serious fall here. He fell on a slippery rock and badly cut his arm.'

'Well, that makes me feel better for being a wuss. Are we making much progress?'

'We'll be out of the canyon soon and then it's pretty much flat and downhill all the way to camp.'

I was relieved to hear Gil say this. Twenty-four kilometres was a tough introduction back to hiking after a rest day. It had been a sluggish start leaving the hostel that morning. When the alarm had gone off, it wasn't just the nerves about getting back on the trail that had made it hard to get going, but also a dense tiredness which was clawing at me to stay in bed. I was sleeping in a different place most nights, always on the move, always planning the next step and pushing myself endlessly to stay motivated and moving. The weariness of a long-term traveller creeping up on me day by day.

Setting off, it had felt like the first day on the trail. My pack, now the heaviest it had ever been at over sixteen kilos in weight, felt awkward again on my hips and shoulders. My boots felt bigger than I remembered them and my body was so cumbersome it was like the five hundred kilometres I'd walked to this point had counted for nothing.

We had made our way to the edge of the city, empty except for a few early risers, and stood on the exit road to Arad on Route 31 opposite a sign pointing west for Tel Aviv and east for the Dead Sea. We'd taken the almost hidden path straight ahead, back into the red and orange vastness where Mount Kina was waiting, our first ascent of the day.

Leaving Nahal Kanfan behind, we now hit a gravel path where we fell into a silent walk, me in the front and Gil behind. *This is it*, I kept thinking, *I'm in the desert*. The sheer scale of the Negev was instant and stifling. If you'd said 'desert' to me before I would have conjured up an image of sand dunes. The Negev, though, is rocky and tough, with towering mountains and deep, winding wadis. It's intimidating, magnificent and relentlessly dry and hot. It was also wonderfully quiet. There were no birds chirping, no rustling of trees, just the gentle scuff of our footsteps. I breathed in the space and let the openness of the nature around me sink in, embracing both the excitement and fear I felt about it.

Shortly afterwards, two small boys, maybe eight years old, passed us riding donkeys. They were both wearing matching Nike tracksuits that were worn grey and full of holes. I recognised them as Bedouin and assumed they were heading towards the small Bedouin settlement we'd passed near the start of the day on Mount Kina. The settlement consisted of no more than a handful of houses made from a mishmash of concrete, corrugated iron, perspex roofing and plastic signage, most of them with large aerials and solar panels sticking out of the roofs, along with a mix of 'for sale' and road signs. The ground around the houses was littered with falling-apart cars and piles of detritus and, apart from a pack of camels, there'd been not a soul in sight.

The Negev Bedouin are Arab tribes who live in the desert in Israel. Although they are traditionally pastoral nomadic, they were forced to settle during the establishment of the Israeli state and, like many nomadic communities in the world, have struggled to have their rights recognised. They were particularly affected in 1979 when 1,500 square kilometres of the Negev were declared a protected nature reserve, seriously restricting their movements in the area.

I knew very little about the Bedouin community in Israel except what Ilan had told me, a man we'd met in Arad who worked for the

Tamar Center Negev NGO. The charity's main aim is to help the Bedouins, predominantly focusing on improving their circumstances through education. Ilan spent many hours patiently answering all my questions. He told us that Negev Bedouins still keep many of their traditions and that each settlement usually consists of just one family with polygamy still very common. One of the neighbourhoods where he works has thirty-two siblings from three women, and a school solely for the children of a single family.

I found the Bedouins and their way of life fascinating. They adhere to Islam, and despite being a subgroup within the Arab minority, about five to ten percent of Bedouin men still choose to serve in the Israel Defense Forces each year even though this is not mandatory (it is currently only mandatory for Druze, Circassian and Jewish Israelis to serve). Confused by this I had asked Ilan why that was, and he had a few theories. Perhaps because they are fiercely loyal by nature to their land. Or maybe because, despite their mistreatment, there has also been a rise in opportunities, charities and individuals supporting and bettering the lives of Bedouins in recent years. He thought and hoped that maybe these positive relationships were helping to build bridges between communities.

The two boys were watching me curiously as they slowly plodded by on their donkeys. I said hello and then stuck my tongue out when they didn't reply, causing them both to giggle. As they passed Gil, he gave them a handful of sweets from his pocket which they squabbled over until they were out of sight.

As so much of the Negev is made up of protected reserves, our accommodation was now almost entirely predetermined in designated camping spaces. We almost missed that night's camping spot, which had been marked out by a circle of rocks and nothing else. As soon as we arrived, I pulled out our phone and turned it on, anxious to test out the water caching system for the first time. Water had been on my mind all day and I'd been careful to check my hydration bladder during our breaks to make sure I wasn't drinking too much. The room for error from now on was small and unforgiving.

I pressed play on the video for our first water drop and the camping area popped up on the screen, along with Yanir's feet. He began walking diagonally across the camp. I followed him to a large boulder. In the video he went behind the boulder and moved a couple of football-sized rocks, one of them a distinct bright white, to reveal bottles of water. Sure enough, right in front of me were the recognisable rocks I could see in the video and, beneath them, to my relief, sat the water bottles.

'It worked!' I yelled to Gil, carrying the heavy load back to camp. There were twelve litres in total. Two for drinking and cooking that night and then five litres each for the next day's hike. After we refilled our own containers, and used what we needed for cooking, we returned the empty bottles to the hiding place for Yanir to collect when he did a water drop for the next hiker.

It was darker much earlier than we were used to as the clocks had moved forward just a few days before. I threw on all the warm clothing I had and started to prepare dinner, wiping my hands on my trousers to get the worst of the dirt off, a level of hygiene that would have once disgusted me but now seemed perfectly normal. I chopped up some tomatoes and cucumber and sprinkled them with salt, the last fresh food we would be having for five days.

A movement caught my eye. A dusty orange fox was trotting across the valley floor in our direction. Despite there being plenty of space to pass, the fox crossed in front of us, cutting right between Gil and I. She held up her head, bushy tail upright, large ears pointed up and slim, cunning eyes looking forward. As she passed, she slowed down, not once looking at either of us, as if making a point that she was not bothered by our presence. This was clearly her territory.

'What a cocky bugger,' I said when she was out of sight. 'I didn't know there were foxes in the desert.'

I thought back to all the foxes we used to see in our street in London and marvelled at how a creature can adapt to thrive in such different environments. I often wouldn't look twice at a passing fox as I made my way home to our Putney flat, in a city where they are labelled as pests, but here, in the wild, it seemed like a gift to have seen her. For the rest of the evening I kept glancing around, hoping to catch one more glimpse of her before bed, but without luck.

It was the middle of the night when Gil woke me with a nudge in my back. I ignored him at first but then started to get irritated as he began rustling the carrier bag, making it hard for me to drift off back to sleep. We only had one carrier bag with us; it was filled with food supplies as our stuff sack hadn't been big enough to carry everything we needed for this six-day stretch. Before sleeping, I had tucked it safely by my feet. It was strange that he had woken in the middle of the night for food, but he must just have been really hungry.

By now half-asleep, I was woken again by further rustling, followed by another firm nudge in my side. *For goodness' sake!* I reluctantly opened my eyes and was about to tell Gil to quit knocking me when I stopped short. The moonlight was providing enough light that I could make out Gil in the tent, lying across from me, fast asleep. I blinked for a few seconds trying to make sense of the situation before concluding that I must've been imagining it all. I lay back down and closed my eyes. That's when I felt another firm push, this time right on my shoulder.

'AARRRGGGHH!' I yelled, jumping sideways into Gil and scrambling to grab my head torch.

'What is it? What is it?' Gil sat up startled, panic in his voice. Locating the torch, I pressed the button to turn on the light and pointed it in the direction of where I'd been pushed. I was expecting to see someone crouched there but was relieved when all my light illuminated was the surrounding rocks and a bushy tail quickly disappearing behind the nearest boulder.

'It's the fox! It's just the fox,' I said, placing my hand on my chest as if to steady my beating heart. 'It was trying to get into the tent. It bloody nudged me. I thought it was you.'

'Yeah, I heard the rustling. I assumed it was you getting food,' Gil said, still looking a bit wide-eyed and shocked by my sudden outburst. Pulling on my boots, without any socks and without doing up the laces, I shuffled around the tent with the torch to inspect for any damage. I was worried that her claws may have torn the fabric, but was relieved that everything looked unscathed apart from a series of grubby paw prints. Before returning to my sleeping bag, still warm from my body heat, I moved the food bag so it was in between us.

'So much for looking forward to uninterrupted nights now we are in the desert,' I said, causing us both to laugh. We might have been away from people, but now the wildlife was joining in the running joke of our interrupted nights. To this point, I could only recall one night on the trail that we had made it a full night with only wee breaks. There was always something or someone to disturb us, or, more frequently, Gil waking me in the night. We'd both noted how intense and vivid our dreams had become on the trail, and this had turned into sleep talking for Gil, who on one night had even yelled out 'HEY!' I woke to find him leaning over me, his own eyes glassy and unseeing. The next morning he told me he had dreamt that someone had pinched my bum.

This was not a journey of restfulness and I'd resigned myself to this. Uninterrupted sleep would come one day, but for now catnaps, in the rare pockets of shade found in the desert beside lone trees or boulders, would have to do.

* * * *

The next day everything was lighter, and the nerves had lifted slightly. We'd completed our first day in the desert, and I'd managed the load of my bag and the scrambles without any falls. We'd found water and camped successfully overnight. Now I just had to continue this on repeat for a month and I would have crossed the Negev desert.

The mugginess in the air told me it was going to be an especially hot day, made worse by us starting later than normal. When the Casio beeped us awake at 5.30am, I turned it off without opening my eyes and mumbled to Gil to ignore it, both relishing an extra hour in bed following the middle-of-the-night fox incident. It meant, though, that we would now need to hike through the heat of the day.

Most of the day was made up of muscle-pumping climbs up and knee-jerking climbs down. With eight kilometres left to go, the ground finally flattened out and we found ourselves on another never-ending path. I started thinking about what I would write in my blog that night, distracting myself to help me through the last hours of the day, which were often the hardest. Now that we were in the desert, signal had become even more sporadic and my postings less frequent. A couple of days previously I'd received a comment on my post from someone I didn't know.

Are you OK? I saw you haven't posted for a couple of days. I hope nothing has happened?!

The idea that someone was checking my blog regularly enough that they would notice I had skipped a day, and even felt compelled to leave a message, was beyond flattering. Did they find my journals entertaining or inspiring? Informative or interesting? It didn't really matter to me; all that mattered was that someone, somewhere was choosing to read them. A throwaway comment like this may not have meant much to the poster, but to me it was another validation of my writing. My readership at this point was moving from dozens into the hundreds and, for the first time, I started to allow myself the confidence to imagine that maybe, just maybe, my blog might take off and open up all sorts of opportunities. I knew that many bloggers had made a career for themselves through their writing and imagining what this might look like was one of my more yummy daydreams. Was it really possible for me to make a career out of something I loved doing so much?

Still when people asked me what I did for a living I replied that I was a teacher, although I didn't feel like one. I never had done. Before leaving for the hike, I'd completed one year of teacher training, focusing on media and film studies for secondary and college-age students. It had been a massive disappointment, filled with constraints, paperwork, disciplining and very little actual teaching. Within a month of starting the course, I knew I'd made a mistake and had not, as I had hoped, finally found the career I'd been endlessly searching for.

In my teenage years I had tried every job imaginable, from being a shop assistant and cold-calling to nannying and teaching drums. Then I moved on to editing films, working in summer camps and assisting in children's nurseries. I loved the independence, the hard work and obsessively watching my savings account go up, but I came to hate every job. I found them tiring, boring and stifling. Mostly, though, I hated working in systems that were inefficient and pointless, without having the freedom to do anything about them. My adult years, after leaving university in search of a career, had been no different. I had landed my first full-time job in a travel company, working in operations.

'We don't take breaks, we just eat from our desks,' my boss said on the first day of work, showing me into her living room which doubled as the small office from where the company was run. I didn't realise then that working ten hours a day without a break wasn't normal. Or that having a boss who loses her temper and micromanages to the level of obsession wasn't acceptable or professional. One day she'd even thrown a stapler at the wall in anger, not far from where I was sitting, because I'd forgotten to get the name of an assistant on the phone who was helping us fix our broken internet connection. She was a bully, and six months in that job was six months too long.

I moved on to a PA and office manager job for a consulting firm, which I knew I'd hate, although at least I never had to contend with any stationery being thrown my way. I lasted two years before changing to a couple of jobs in the charity sector, the last of which came with yet another infuriating micromanaging boss, along with spending habits and office behaviours that were so far from charitable it made me boil with anger. So I switched to teaching. By this point, massively dissatisfied and deflated, I was feeling the slow chipping away at a part of myself that was getting harder to protect.

By now, I had a reputation as someone who couldn't hold down a job. I don't know at what age it stops being cute that you want to try lots of things, but I was clearly way past that point. Switching jobs so much wasn't a sign of healthy curiosity, it was irresponsible. I should have stayed in my jobs longer, I should have stayed in the same industry, I should have found a career and stuck with it, climbing that ladder everyone talks about. It shouldn't have surprised me, therefore, that when I told people I was taking a break from my job to hike the length of Israel, they weren't full of excitement for me as I'd naively hoped. Instead, most focused on the one thing I was trying to escape. *Aren't you worried about how it will look on your CV? That you'll become unemployable? You're both in good jobs, don't you think it's better to stick them out?*

I had found escape, though, and the break from societal constraints that I had been craving. Despite its struggles, the trail had been all I had hoped it would be in this sense. It was moments like this, where I had the freedom to think creatively and the time to daydream about future possibilities for myself, that I found some self-forgiveness. London had been so noisy and closed-in and life had been a juggling act of busyness. No wonder I hadn't been able to work out what I wanted to do.

'What the... is that a conveyor belt? It's huge,' I said to Gil, my career daydreams snapping back to the desert. Up ahead in the distance was a metal bridge cutting through the mountains on either side and stretching the length of the wide valley in between.

'Yeah, it's transporting minerals from the Dead Sea to the factories. Potassium, I think.'

As we neared it I could see the conveyor belt wasn't working but the ground was littered with bright red sediments that had fallen off and scattered. I didn't recognise what the mineral was but it looked toxic and like it didn't belong here.

'Why don't they just put the factory closer?'

'They decided to ban factories next to the Dead Sea. I was reading in the guide last night that belts like these take the minerals to an industrial zone called Zafit.'

'How long does it go on for?'

'Eighteen kilometres, apparently.'

My mouth dropped open. I couldn't get my head around the fact that this monstrosity cut through so much desert. Who'd allowed such a thing to happen? It seemed criminal.

'Mad, isn't it?' Gil said quietly. 'They can never undo this.'

I was desperate to get away from the machinery but my attempts to escape the destruction were short-lived as around the corner was a working quarry and, just metres from its entrance, our designated campsite. Neither Gil nor I dropped our backpacks as we normally did when we arrived to camp. Instead, we surveyed the scene around us. Menacing machinery and moving vehicles, visible beyond the factory walls, made a horrendous noise that seemed like torture to my ears in the otherwise silent desert. The walls and tall structures were a metallic scar on nature. That wasn't the only thing. The campsite was a dumping ground, littered with old tyres, plastic waste, toilet paper and burnt debris, a rotten smell instantly reaching my nose.

'This is disgusting,' Gil said, looking around and mindlessly kicking at a bit of discarded rubber by his feet.

'I'm not staying here.'

'Where else can we sleep? We aren't meant to camp in the reserve.'

I pulled out the map. 'I think if we camp at the top of this hill we'll still be outside the border. And we'll be considerate campers like always. Leave no trace. It's getting dark soon and we'll be gone early.'

Gil was quiet for a moment, thinking of his options. 'I guess it's fine for one night. It's not very clear but if we do get caught we might be fined.'

'I'm happy to take the risk.'

We found our cached water and lugged the heavy bottles up the hill. At the top, to the side of the track, we found a suitable flat spot. We were still close enough to hear the quarry but at least it was out of sight. After dinner, I decided to take a walk in my sandals to the edge of the hill to see the view on the other side. I took purposeful, long strides, gently stretching my hips as I went. They were permanently stiff but had reached new levels of discomfort the day before when, the morning after the fox encounter, I'd woken up with such pain in my hip joints that I'd barely been able to move. It was like I'd aged fifty years overnight and my body had given up on me. Rolling inelegantly on to my stomach I'd managed to manoeuvre myself on to all fours where I could sit up more easily. My roll mat had deflated. This had been happening frequently since the Helicopter Incident on day two of the trail, which had showered all our items with tiny thorns that we were still finding to this day. Despite locating the holes in the roll mat and covering them with the repair kit we'd brought with us, there always seemed to be more. Gil and I didn't have designated mats. They were both stuffed into the bag and pulled out at random but somehow I seemed to keep drawing the short straw and landing on the one that would deflate.

When I reached the drop-off the view was even more spectacular than I had anticipated. Nothing but mountains and valleys of orange as far as the eye could see and, above them, as if to ensure that I give the landscape my full attention, a setting sun painting them with a vibrant glow. As I did with all the views I tried to take a mental snapshot, to imprint it on my mind forever, although I knew that within a few days the memory would fade, the true grandeur of the space reserved only for the immediate moment. I felt a tingle of anticipation at the thought of heading into such a stunning and adventurous setting the following morning. From hiking level it was always hard to grasp the scale of the mountains around us.

I'd brought the Red Book with me so I could study the map covering the next few days, every hiker's obsession. Perching myself on a convenient pile of rocks I pulled back the pages, opening my second hiking companion. The dirt, creases and dog-eared pages told the story of our journey. It was the reason we couldn't bring ourselves to tear the pages as we went, burning what we no longer needed. This was a common technique used by hikers, even mentioned in the introduction of the guide, to help reduce the weight of their load.

Inside the book was a note and signature left by Jacob Saar, the author of the guide. Gil had contacted him to ask some questions in advance of our hike and, as the trail passed not far from his house, shortly before it reached Jerusalem, he had kindly offered to put us up for a night. He was the perfect host. When we arrived at his house, which had the three trail waymarker stripes painted on the stairs to his porch, he handed us a plate of snacks and showed us the shower.

'We'll talk more at dinner,' he said, giving us enough time to ease our hunger, stretch and freshen up in new clothes in peace. This was a man who knew all too well the burning desires of a hiker at the end of a long day; as you would expect, as he had hiked the trail four times. It was his passion and the thing we talked most about all evening. Our experiences on the trail, how it had changed over the years, the route constantly adapting as obstacles are fed back or new builds approved, and how he came to write the guide. The next day, as he waved us off with a bag full of snacks and lunch, I felt I was saying goodbye to a dear friend who I'd known a lot longer than just a day. Hardly surprising, as Jacob and his words had been with me every step of the way.

Before heading back to rejoin Gil I flicked back to one of the book's first pages, which showed a full map of the Israel National Trail, the line meandering its way the length of the long, narrow country. I followed the line to roughly where I thought we were, noticing how little distance it looked like we had left to cover. For the first time, the line ahead was shorter than the one behind. Although we had passed the halfway mark some days ago, I hadn't allowed myself much time to think about it. Mostly this was because I couldn't even humour the thought of turning around and covering all that distance again, but now we were past it, with some long walking days behind us, the end all of a sudden didn't feel so far away. There was some certainty, a quiet confidence that I knew I was going to be successful in what I'd set out to achieve. There was no more space in my mind to contemplate quitting. Instead, that space was now filled with trying to work out what would come next. It was a big question mark which hung over our hike and, with the end point always seeming so impossibly far away, I had been able to pay it no attention until now. It couldn't stay unanswered forever, though. Would we return to London? What would we do for work? Was I ready to face reality again? Was this enough?

I took a deep and intentional breath and looked across the horizon once more, catching the last slither of sun as it slid behind the mountain range. I had a lot of questions still unanswered and, thankfully, a huge desert where I could try to work them out.

Chapter 9

I realised I'd made a mistake pushing my bag in front of me rather than dragging it from behind. Crouched on all fours, shuffling forward, the gravel cutting into my bare knees, I edged my way onwards in the claustrophobic tunnel. I felt like I was doing some sort of drill in an army training camp.

Crawling through tunnels had become a regular occurrence on the trail as a way of passing safely under railway tracks or impassable obstacles. The tunnels were obviously an afterthought as they were always very small, usually never more than a metre or so wide and high.

I was currently halfway through the longest one yet, forty metres in length, cursing the people who had built it, wishing they'd allowed just a bit more space to make it that bit easier to pass. To save my legs from getting any more cuts, I lifted my knees so I was balancing on my hands and feet in a plank position, moving one hand and foot at a time. I only managed a few small steps like this before intense cramp sent shooting pain into my hip. Yelling out, I instinctively turned and straightened my leg and, in doing so, whacked my head full pelt on the concrete roof.

'OW!'

'Are you alright?' Gil's voice echoed from the darkness ahead, already free of the tunnel.

'Cramp!' I managed in between gritted teeth.

Once the pain had ebbed I began shuffling myself forward but barely made it another metre before I had to stop again, massaging my tight muscle to try and help the cramp pass. I heard a scuffling sound up ahead before a head torch appeared over the top of my bag.

'I'll take your backpack,' Gil said, dragging it away from me. Without having to worry about the bag I was able to follow without further incident, although for good measure I did whack my head on the ceiling one more time as I straightened up on exiting the tunnel.

Ahead of us loomed the menacing climb of Snapir Gadol; translated, this means 'Large Flipper', although I couldn't see a flipper no matter which way I looked. Sitting at its base was a large group of older hikers, the first people we'd seen in three days. We tentatively made our way through the crowd, stepping over their bags. Just as we were close to breaking free, a tall, broad man with a large white bushy beard came striding over to us, hand outstretched.

'Dany,' he said, with a firm shake. I noticed he was wearing a headset microphone, the cable running to a small speaker which was strapped to his belt.

'As in Dany Gaspar?' Gil asked.

'That's me.' We'd heard of Dany via Jacob and other hikers we'd passed along the way. He was considered a legend on the trail, holding the record for the most amount of times anyone has hiked the INT: seventeen to date. He had worked with the committee responsible for developing it, personally determining many of the pathways the route now takes.

'Are you guiding this group?' I asked him once we'd finished our introductions.

'Yes, I spend most of my year guiding people on the INT these days and the rest of my time hiking other trails overseas. Most of this group are walking the full trail but only one section at a time. We take it slow. We take a lot of breaks and talk of the land and history around us. And are you walking the full trail in one go?' he asked.

'Yes, we are,' I said, eager to have the approval of such a hiking legend.

Dany's hand went to his side and the portable speaker, and clicked a button. His other hand moved the microphone closer to his mouth.

'This is Bex and Gil,' his voice boomed through the speaker and the crowd hushed – although not entirely, I noted. I'd seen guides use these portable speakers in Israel before, even teachers, but for a hiking group it seemed a little comical as, apart from this chatty bunch, there was no noise to compete with.

'They are walking the full length of the Israel National Trail,' Dany said.

'Oooooooh,' the crowd called out, '*kol hakavod*,' well done, eyes on us as we stood beside Dany as if we were being presented to the class.

'They walk an average of twenty-five kilometres a day and carry all their own camping gear.' More *ohs* and *ahs* followed. 'This is the size of the rucksack you need for doing a multi-day hike.' Dany pointed at our packs and I turned slightly so they could see my bag. Covering the microphone with his hand Dany turned to us. 'What's in this plastic bag attached to the outside?'

'Just our rubbish we're carrying out,' Gil replied.

Speaking into the microphone again, Dany said, 'In this bag is all their litter. They carry all their own rubbish away with them, leaving nothing behind.' This time we even got a spattering of applause.

We stayed with Dany and the group a little longer, answering questions about our hike. It was fun being the centre of such praise but we needed to keep moving. Shaking hands once more with Dany we wished the hikers all good luck, many of them patting the backs of our bags or shoulders as we passed. Aware of the eyes on us as we left, I walked away with purposeful confidence, as if I'd spent my whole life just casually strolling across deserts.

* * * *

The next morning I sat in my tent munching on walnuts and raisins, willing myself to move. I stared, unfocused, at nothing, my head torch illuminating the green nylon cover of the tent. We'd started putting up the outer part of the tent religiously now to help combat the drastic drop in temperatures that hit us every night. The extra layer was exceptionally thin, but made a surprising difference when it came to keeping us warm, the heat of our bodies creating a snug cocoon that stayed cosy until the zip door was opened.

Last night the outer layer had also served another purpose, as it had hidden the view of the campsite. I'd been pretty disheartened to find that our camp for the night was next to yet another industrial factory, this time a phosphate chemical plant. With no other suitable camping options within close distance, we had put up the tent with reluctance and a bit of moaning. It was hard to stay mad for long, though, as a security guard from the factory generously gave us cartons of orange juice and a tray of pre-packaged food from their canteen, and even offered to take our bag of rubbish away. I had to remind myself of this generosity when, at one in the morning, we were both woken with a scare after an immense noise exploded from within the factory walls. A few seconds later, an invisible force of air punched through us, shaking the tent and catching my breath as it passed. That wasn't the worst of it, though. Just as we had got over the shock of being woken in such an abrupt way, a cloud of dust reached us, seeping through the gaps under the tent, rising like smoke and sending us both into coughing fits. The rest of the night I slept with a buff over my mouth and nose.

'We should get going, Bexi, if we want to get to the top for sunrise,' Gil called to me from outside the tent. I knew he was right, so I piled in one more mouthful of food and then began the task of getting myself clothed and my bag packed. I would never normally eat breakfast before leaving camp but today I had woken up feeling ravenous despite our late-night snack, although it crossed my mind that maybe it was just nerves.

The day had finally come for us to climb Mount Karbolet. It had been playing on our minds since we had left Arad and, although I was nervous about the task ahead, I also felt relieved that finally the day was here. From tomorrow, the looming presence of this mountain would no longer have to occupy my thoughts.

I'd read and reread the description for today's hike in the Red Book, making sure I hadn't missed any important bits of information. There were three parts to the day. Step one was leaving the chemical plant behind and climbing to the top of Karbolet. From here we kept height on a knife-edge as we made our way along a relentless stream of ascents and descents for most of the day. The final stage, the part that made me most anxious, was the descent from the mountain through a wadi, called Nahal Afran, which included both steep and difficult scrambles.

The warning in the Red Book for the day ahead was clear:

> *You will be hiking at a slow pace, sometimes less than 1km/hr. The descent in Nahal Afran is even slower. Many hikers have been caught in the dark in the last 500 meters of Nahal Afran, the slowest section of the day…* ***Under no circumstances should you hike in Nahal Afran after dark.***

The book had both bolded and underlined the last sentence. There was only one other example in the book when a warning had warranted both:

Do not cross the railroad by crossing over the track!

The fact that the hike in the Nahal Afran was comparable in danger to being hit by a train did little to reassure me. I rarely enjoyed scrambling, especially if it was on a descent, when I was unable to relax with the constant awareness that there was a fall below me. I'd never been afraid of heights, but that didn't mean I enjoyed hanging off the edge of potential fatal drops, the only things preventing me from falling the grip of my hand and my clumsy footing. This was always made worse by the presence of my rucksack, its weight and size a burden on my body.

I hurled that burden on to my back, now considerably lighter at least as we only had two days' worth of food supplies left. After doing up the clips and putting my hands through the straps on my walking poles, I paused for a moment. A light, crisp breeze tickled my face. The weather forecast said it would be thirty degrees today but that seemed like an age away. Now, pre-dawn, it was cold, so cold that I had my fleece and beanie on and longed for the snugness of my sleeping bag. Up ahead Gil was making his way along the path, his torchlight illuminating a triangle in front of him. I lifted my hand to turn my own headtorch off. Above me was a full moon and an audience of stars, providing enough light for me to see the way ahead. As if making a point of marking this moment, a shooting star cut across the sky.

It took an hour for us to reach the top of Karbolet, the face of the mountain towering above us. The stars were now out of sight, replaced by the beginning of a light-blue clear sky. At the top, we stopped to take a break. The trail stretched out ahead of us along the infamous rolling knife-edge of Karbolet. It was, without question, the most beautiful view of the trail so far. On both sides there was nothing but wide-open spaces, mountains and us, alone, perched on the side of one of them. The sun peeked over the horizon, blinding us with its glow. It lit up the mountainsides and caused dramatic shadows to fall across the canyons.

'Wow,' said Gil.

'Seriously, wow.'

Within minutes of the sun making an appearance, I was peeling off my fleece and tugging the beanie from my head. My skin tingled in anticipation of the heat we would soon be facing. The forecast had told us it was going to be the hottest day of the week. It was a cruel coincidence that it should land on such a tough day.

It was time to get going. Today was not a day for long breaks but a day to keep our legs moving. The guide had called each of the many climbs we would have to tackle today both 'difficult and strenuous' and I could not think of a more accurate description. To our right was a sheer and sudden drop into the crater. To our left, a more sloping drop-off. We were stuck in between them with no pathway to follow, just jagged rocks on the knife-edge to navigate. There was no switching off or daydreaming, as this type of terrain required my full concentration to make sure each step found a safe home. It entailed hours of effort where our phrase 'what goes down must come up' was very much being put into practice. Each time we were up over a peak, a new one would come into view ahead, but not before we had to drop down and undo all the height that we had just gained.

I was tense. Tense from the fear of tripping and the level of concentration this type of hiking required. Tense from the knowledge that we were nearing Nahal Afran. Tense from noticing the time ticking away and that we had only a limited amount of light left before reaching the most dangerous part of our day. We'd left even earlier than usual and were carefully following the guide, which timed each section, to ensure we didn't push on if there was no chance we were going to make it in time. I hoped it would be enough.

With all that preying heavily on my mind, I had to force myself to stop once in a while, making sure that I wasn't forgetting to eat and to keep my body fuelled. Drinking regularly was equally important. We were carrying six litres each and needed every drop to replace the sweat from hiking. Even more so as we were high up on an exposed ridge meaning there was no break from the sun all day, its blinding presence impossible to escape.

The trail, at last, veered left. This was where we would begin the descent into Nahal Afran. We both sat on the ground and calculated, just to double-check, that there was still enough time to start the climb down safely. The guide had made clear that if we weren't sure we'd make it that we should detour and get off the mountain at a different point.

'We can do it. Maybe even with an hour to spare,' Gil said. I was about to ask how he was doing but stopped myself. His body was slumped back against the bag, eyes darting about nervously, his top soaked through and all his visible skin glistening with sweat. Sometimes it was better not to check in with yourself.

Our hiking sticks were folded down and attached to the backs of our rucksacks to free our hands. We clambered through dry pools and over boulders, and rock-climbed down drops. We took each section one step at a time, taking it in turns to manoeuvre over the most difficult of parts. It had been hard to imagine how hiking could slow to less than one kilometre per hour but now I could understand why. My thigh muscles were shaking, my knees throbbing, suffering from the downward scrambles, and my lips and hands were cracked. The climb through Nahal Afran was nothing shot of brutal.

When I took the final step off the mountain I let out a sigh. We had made it to the base of Karbolet. I couldn't celebrate, though, not yet. I still had an hour of walking ahead before we reached the campsite. This should have been an easy stretch, entirely on the flat, which is why I hadn't given it any thought, but it was an excruciating hour. The terrain looked like we had landed on Mars, with black rocks scattered across the floor, their sharp points battering the soles of my feet which were, by now, bruised and swollen. The sun was setting, but the heat from the day had already done its damage. My skin was raw from exposure, stinging from sunburn. I was drained, with no energy left to even think or make a decision. As was always the case on a hot day, I didn't have much of an appetite, but I scooped more snacks into my mouth, hopeful they would give me a modicum of energy to reach camp.

Eventually, we made it. There were no congratulations or relief as every fibre of my body was screaming to rest. Like robots we carried out the tasks that needed to be done before we could sleep. We collected our hidden water, put up the tent and ate some pasta with a side of painkillers. I crawled into my sleeping bag feeling exhausted, an empty shell.

When I woke the next day my knees were so stiff that I could barely get myself out of the tent. Using a walking pole I righted myself and took a few steps, warming up the joints and feeling the stiffness easing as I moved. Apart from my knees, my body had recovered relatively well.

Later that day we passed two day hikers who asked us if we had heard the news.

'What news?' Gil asked back.

'Trump won the election yesterday.' We hadn't heard the news. In fact, neither of us had even known the election was happening. We hadn't checked the news since we started the hike. What was happening in the 'real' world seemed so detached and unimportant. All that mattered to me now was the weather forecast and the map showing the way ahead. While the world watched on in anticipation, glued to their screens, I was up a mountain in the desert learning what it meant to reach my limits.

It was jarring to be taken back to the world outside our trail. The one filled with politics, media and negativity. I much preferred staying in my hiker's bubble. The one where tomorrow would be a blissful rest day, Trump was irrelevant and I had completed a seven-day stretch in the desert and the hardest day on the entire trail.

Chapter 10

On both sides of us tall crags towered above, almost vertical, boxing us in. The valley floor was wide and flat. Turning another corner, I spotted something up ahead that initially made me think I must be hallucinating. Nestled in among the dry, rocky terrain was an explosion of greenery and, right in the centre of the oasis, Ein Akev spring. It was a perfect bowl carved out in the smooth rock, the water the same green as the trees that surrounded it. Above the spring on the vertical crag a wall of plants spilled over the top of the mountain like a waterfall.

You could be mistaken into thinking there is no life to be found in the barren landscape of the desert, but each day brought something new. Sometimes it might be a creature hidden and camouflaged, easy to miss, like a gecko or a snake, and sometimes something glaringly obvious like this hub of flora and fauna.

Nearing the trees, I noticed the temperature drop a few degrees instantly, a cool moisture hanging in the air. Rich palms and Euphrates poplars towered over us and reeds scratched at our legs. Sunlight shimmered and danced on the water's surface. Gil rushed past me, ditching his bag. He stripped off his clothes and made his way to the edge of the smooth rock, where there was a sudden drop-off into the water. He paused before doing an exaggerated jump, fully submerging himself.

'Damn, that's cold!' he said, shooting back out of the water with a shriek. 'You coming in?'

'Just my legs.' I was so sluggish that even the thought of undressing and redressing seemed like a task too big. Instead, I pulled off my boots and socks, rolled up my shorts and lay on the edge in the sun, slowly lowering my legs into the water. Gil was right, it was freezing, and I shuddered at the cold against my skin. I lay back on my pack, closing my eyes against the bright sun. The top of my body too hot, and the bottom too cold.

Gil ducked and dived in the water, playing the way a child would in a pool. It reminded me of when we'd first met while travelling, and a fun-loving Gil who I'd not seen for a while.

My breathing slowed, the sluggishness in my body pulling me backwards into sleep, until a desert resident snatched what could have been a long and peaceful rest. I felt the unbearable sensation of tiny feet crawling on the exposed skin on my arm. I wafted the fly away, then scratched at the itch it left behind. A few moments later I felt the same sensation but this time on the end of my nose, then on my arm again, then on my ear. No matter how much I wafted, they always returned. Waiting in anticipation of where the next fly was going to land was intolerable.

The huge desert flies were ruthless and had become our permanent companions since we began hiking in the Negev. Throughout the day, dozens of them would gather on our bags and clothes. 'Hitchhikers', I'd started calling them, as they'd find a spot and stay there sometimes for hours as we walked. I didn't mind them grabbing a lift, as long as they weren't touching me, but us stopping and settling in for a rest always seemed to be their cue to start bothering us.

'Arrrggghh,' I yelled out in frustration, my swatting becoming a bit more frantic.

'You know that won't help.'

'I know,' I said, now using my hat to try to stun some of them. 'I. Just. Hate. FLIES.'

I started drying my feet huffily with my shawl then passed it to Gil as he got out. My only salvation on days like this was knowing that at least once the tent was up I could hide in the netting, free from any crawling legs.

Making my way up out of the valley, my leg muscles were still pulsing slightly from their submersion in cold water. Suddenly, a sour stench hit the back of my throat, causing me to gag. Just to the side of the path was the rotting carcass of an animal, only a few bones and tufts of hair remaining. The curved horns were undoubtedly from an ibex. Despite the smell, the freshness of the blood seeping into the ground led me to believe that the animal had died recently. My initial thought was that the ibex must have been attacked, but there was nothing left in the area, other than humans, that would pose such a threat. The Negev had once been home to many big cats, but the last remaining, the Arabian leopards, had been considered extinct since 2017 due to human activity. My best guess was that this unfortunate ibex had taken a fatal fall and provided a feast for the vultures we occasionally saw circling overhead.

Reaching the top of the climb, I looked down and spotted the second oasis of the day, Ein Shaviv. Water from the surrounding cliffs filtered down into the huge basin, creating the perfect environment for plants to thrive. It was like someone had drawn a large shape on the rocky floor and planted it with a hundred trees, all clumped together, a complete contrast from the rest of the stark terrain. The INT snaked down the cliff and across the basin, cutting straight through the trees. Beyond that were more mountains, more canyons, continuing undisturbed until everything faded out on the horizon. The views just kept coming, one after the other, never with an end in sight. A barren desert that felt like it went on forever.

I stopped to catch my breath from the strenuous climb, until a fly flew straight into my ear. I swatted at it, shaking my head, then reluctantly carried on.

* * * *

As the layers of dust thickened on my skin, the days in the desert passed by, my stripped-back, simple existence all merging into a strange passing of time. I finally had the thinking space I had always imagined the trail would give me. It didn't come in calm moments of enlightenment or new-found wisdom, but stemmed from pure boredom. Although I was relishing the challenge and felt endless gratitude for the landscapes that rolled before me, there was no denying that hiking was monotonous. Plodding forward hour after hour, day after day, with loneliness and isolation becoming more constant, hiking swung from wonderfully exhilarating to tediously bland. I was grateful to have Gil with me, not for safety as most people assumed, but for companionship. Still, our conversations dried up and we found ourselves spending more time hiking apart, each of us at our own pace, looking for ways to occupy our minds. I yearned for the distraction of a busy coffee shop or the crowds of London, a people-watcher's paradise.

Up to this point, much of my mind had been preoccupied with nothing but the loud demands of my most basic needs. There was no space for pondering when all I could think about was how hungry I was, how hot I felt, how much discomfort I was in. Hiking was still tough, that hadn't gone away, but my body had adapted to the heat, my muscles strengthening by the day. I was getting comfortable with being uncomfortable and that freed my mind, which was now as vast as the space around me. I had infinite hours to think, or perhaps it was infinite hours to listen.

As I walked, a montage of random memories would play out in my head. Sometimes these were significant moments from my life: my teacher telling me it was my fault I was getting teased because I had cut my hair short and 'wasn't acting like a normal girl'; opening my GCSE results to surprisingly good grades; my parents separating; the last conversation with a friend before she took her own life, those few words forever played on repeat like a broken record; laying eyes on Gil as he walked into Spanish Conversation Club; catching my grandad Stanley looking at me in a way I couldn't make sense of until I heard he had passed a few days later; stopping by a tree in the New Forest and Gil producing a ring from his pocket.

Sometimes, though, the memories were so random it amazed me that my mind had made the effort to store them, like the excitement of finding a four-leaf clover in my junior school playground but having no-one around to show, or my Grandad Fred teaching me to draw a house in three dimensions and me noticing the colouring on his fingernails from decades of smoking.

Often I'd return to the same point in time, a few years before doing the hike, when I had been my most unhappy, consumed with a cloud of hopelessness and depression brought on by the struggles of moving to an isolated city with Gil, bad jobs and financial strain. I had thought that being spat into the world of adulthood, no longer with a home and a bed that I could call my own, thanks to the breakdown of my family, was as lost as I would ever feel, but I was wrong. Nothing had been more disorientating and shattering than losing my way internally as I battled with poor mental health.

In the desert, though, I could feel old wounds being healed. For a short time, I stopped worrying about finding my way in life or questioning my every move; the path ahead clearly marked by three stripes, the only direction I needed for two months. It was a relief that calmed the turbulence as my compass gradually recentred. Each waymarker pointing south, another step in the right direction.

We had been blessed with days of scenery that belonged on a postcard and, in between them, a rest day in a tiny desert town called Tzofar where we stayed in a Bedouin hut. The place was so slow I could well believe that if I saw a clock the seconds might be ticking backwards. Tzofar was just four streets wide and three streets long, and surrounded by date farms with thousands of date palms lined in perfect rows. We walked through the town to reach the small convenience shop but didn't see anybody along the way. I peered into the houses looking for signs of life but saw none. Perhaps they were all dozing, like the cats and dogs and camels that seemed to be occupying every available shady spot, all coming to the same conclusion that the only way to survive the sweltering days was to sleep through them.

The further we hiked south, away from the cities and villages of the north, the more I started to feel the vastness of the desert and our solitude. Our tiny insignificance had never been more obvious than when we reached the steep drop-off on the edge of the Ramon Crater. The Negev has five craters and the trail passes three: the Small Crater, the Big Crater and Ramon Crater, the largest. I stood on the edge, as close as I dared go, and felt a thrill as blood rushed through my veins, imagining joining the vultures above our heads as they dived into the expanse below. Walking down to the crater floor, through thick fog that was clouding our vision, was a magical start to the days that followed as we weaved our way through wadis; but one of these wadis led me to a terrifying moment. Gil was ahead of me but just in sight and it was one of the few times in the desert we had been walking on sand that wasn't just a thin layer of coating. Each step on the soft, fine sand swallowed my foot, necessitating double the effort and making for painfully slow progress.

Eventually, towards the wadi walls, stretches of gravel offered rocky relief underfoot. So focused was I on my stepping, though, that it took some time for me to look up and realise that I had not seen a trail marker for a while and I could no longer see Gil. I yelled out for him, hoping he might pop his head around one of the turnings ahead to show me the way, but there was no reply. I looked back, seeing that there had been three possible routes through the canyon to this point. Which one had I come through? My instinct told me the furthest left so I backtracked and headed that way. After a while I passed a lone tree sitting in the middle of the canyon, the curve of its branches so distinct I was sure I hadn't seen it before. My chest tightened slightly knowing I was off the trail, so I quickly returned to the crossroads, now walking at a much faster pace. The walk back felt longer than the first time. Was this definitely the way I had come? I reached the crossroads but wasted no time deliberating, and instead took the middle turning. Again, the scenery around me didn't look familiar but I was sure I hadn't come from the turning furthest from the right. I pushed on a little further, feeling my heart race a little and sweat soaking the back of my shirt. The walls around me suddenly seemed taller and the heat in the air just that bit more suffocating. I usually passed by my surroundings without paying a huge deal of attention but now I noticed every detail, each rock, each bare thorny bush. Had I passed that earlier?

I stopped when I reached a sandy section and felt my shoulders drop slightly as I spotted footprints in the sand. To the side was the orange, blue and white striped marker I had missed, indicating that I should turn off and climb out of the wadi up the ten metres or so to the top. It was a reminder that a moment of lapsed concentration could have seriously ill effects.

The incident had shaken me, but not enough that I had lost my confidence to hike sections of the trail on my own. Five days had passed since encountering Ein Akev spring. I was now walking ahead of Gil, listening to 'The Songs of Distant Earth' by Mike Oldfield, an album I adored and couldn't remember the last time I had listened to uninterrupted, when ahead I saw a group of ten or so people gathered around cars. We'd barely seen anyone since leaving Arad, so their presence piqued my interest instantly. I was eager to get close to see what they were doing. I picked up my pace slightly and, as I got nearer, I could see there was a heated discussion going on. The cars were all Land Rovers, lined up on a 4x4 track that took a sharp right turn up a steep and very uneven climb, the same path I needed to take. From where I was standing the track looked impossible for a vehicle to get over.

A yellow Labrador Retriever came bounding up to me, tongue lolling out to one side, and I gave him a scratch behind his ear until his owner called him back, 'Negev!' Not wanting to interrupt the discussions, I gave them a brief greeting as I passed, then walked up the incline, stopping halfway and moving to one side where a ledge provided the perfect place for me to take a break. Watching them from above, I could see a lot of bravado, arms on hips, exaggerated shouting and frantic pointing, without much listening. The group was made up entirely of men, as were almost all the hikers we passed, and as was usually the case when I was outdoors in the UK.

Gil caught up with me and joined me on the ledge.

'What are they fighting about?' I asked, eager to know.

'This climb and the route they need to take to get their cars up it.'

'There's no way you can get a car over this.'

'You definitely can. These jeeps will go over anything.'

'It's so steep and uneven. Look at that massive dip there, how will a car get over that?'

Gil shrugged and we both turned our attention back to the group, where there was movement. One of the men got into the Land Rover at the front and turned on the engine. The rest of them all moved back and the jeep began to edge its way towards the climb.

'There's no way,' I said.

'I bet you the last piece of halva he makes it.'

'Deal.' For both of us, halva had become a much-loved hiking snack: a dense, sweet and horrifically calorific confection made from sesame.

The man drove forward, taking a sharp right, then slowly began to climb over the rocks. The jeep bounced around as the slope got steeper and steeper. The driver looked across at us and lifted his head in smug greeting.

'Move back a bit,' Gil said suddenly, not sounding too sure of the man's abilities. He scooted along the ledge and indicated for me to join him. 'Just in case.'

The jeep climbed up the first half of the incline with relative ease until it was level with us. This was the trickiest part, where the crag steepened very suddenly and opened into a number of large dips. The driver, his tongue out in concentration, slowly revved the engine, the jeep's front left wheel now in the air. The jeep edged onwards, then the wheel caught on to a rock which propelled the vehicle forward. The Land Rover made it up and over, disappearing out of sight. I handed over the last piece of halva to Gil.

The driver appeared at the top of the incline with his hands in his pockets, suddenly wearing a pair of aviators and with a general air of trying really hard to look like that had been no effort at all. He shouted down to the next driver, a man in a bright orange T-shirt, who obediently got into the next jeep in line. There was no strut in this guy's walk and I could see the perspiration on his forehead from where I was sitting. He made the first part of the climb without a problem until he reached the tricky section. He hadn't positioned the jeep correctly so, as he went over the dip, the front wheel didn't catch on to the rock as it was meant to but instead remained in the air. He then made the mistake of revving the jeep forward even further, now causing the back wheel to lose its grip as well, so the vehicle was precariously balancing on two wheels and started to veer backwards in slow motion. We both gasped as it teetered precariously, rocking back and forth like a see-saw.

Mr Aviators ran down the slope and leapt into the air, arms flailing, landing on the front of the bonnet as if his slight weight could make any difference to the 2.5-tonne vehicle. At the same time Negev came bounding up to join him, leaping about, tail wagging, yapping in excitement. Mr Aviators began yelling instructions to the driver, as did all the men gathered below. The orange T-shirt man wiped his forehead, the sweat now dripping. I felt a little guilty for adding the extra pressure of an audience, but there was no way I was leaving now.

The next few minutes were tense. There was lots of revving, wheel spinning and a load more shouting but eventually the front wheel made contact with a rock and the jeep made it over. I let out a big sigh. I hadn't realised I'd been holding my breath.

'Mind if I go on ahead again and see you at camp?' I asked Gil a while later, after we'd watched the rest of the jeeps get over, leaving us once more on our own.

'Sure, I'll see you at camp.'

With my long legs I had a tendency to march at a faster pace than Gil, who was happy to take things a bit slower. We were now walking in the Arava region, an open basin with a wide track and very few features in sight except the mountains off in the distance and the occasional lone dry tree.

The designated camping spot was next to a crag face. Rocks had been placed in a rectangle shape, marking out the space where we were permitted to be. I reached the area and dropped my bag on the first flat section, noticing that something had been left tucked behind the bordering rocks. On closer inspection, I saw a small Tupperware box and on top of it a two-litre bottle of water. I opened the lid to inspect the contents of the box. There was a mix of nuts and raisins and, nestled in between them, brightly coloured chocolate-covered peanut M&Ms. I quickly picked out a few of the sweets and popped them in my mouth before closing the lid and returning the box under the bottle of water. I knew if I didn't practise some self-discipline I'd eat them all before Gil got his fair share.

I didn't know what time it was – Gil tended to wear the watch we'd brought with us – but judging by the sun being high I knew I had at least a few hours to kill before bed. Gil also had the change of clothes in his bag as we'd recently split the way we organised our gear, looking for the most efficient way to pack. It only trimmed a second off our packing time but gave us both great satisfaction in its efficiency.

I was desperate to get out of my sweaty clothes. I could suddenly feel the damp fabric against my hot skin. Not able to bear it any longer, I yanked off my boots and pulled off my outfit until I was just in my underwear. I laid the clothes carefully over my bag to dry in the sun. A big advantage of arriving early was that I wouldn't have to put them on damp in the morning. I tiptoed to a large boulder, which was close to the crag face but far enough away that I didn't have to worry about rockfalls, pulled myself up and laid down on its surface, which was just slightly heated from the day's sun.

Lying on my back, arms outstretched, I soaked up the breeze that brushed my skin, thankful that it seemed to be keeping the flies away. I looked down at my body. It had been such a long time since I'd last seen myself in a mirror. I had a dramatic tan line where my shorts and socks covered my legs, although it was hard to know how much of that was the sun and how much was just layers of dirt. My stomach was flatter. I had red marks on my hips and shoulders where the bag rubbed, rough skin on my feet and dirt under my nails that looked like it would take weeks to scrape out. My legs were covered in hair, sticking out wildly in all directions, but I didn't see that so much; I was too busy admiring the newly defined line where my calf muscle now protruded.

The sound of Bob Marley's 'Three Little Birds' being sung badly reached my ears. Gil appeared on the horizon, headphones in, sticks waving about in an attempt to dance while carrying a big backpack. He stepped up on to the campsite border and jumped down, almost landing on the box of sweets, oblivious to their existence. He pulled out his earphones, a goofy grin on his face.

'What?' I said to him defensively.

'Nothing,' he said, still grinning. 'You're glowing. You should wear that more often.'

With the rest of the afternoon free, I decided to make the most of having the additional water, left by a generous hiker, to clean and organise our gear. I laid out all our items, pulling them from stuff sacks and putting them in neat piles in front of me. There were fewer things than we had started with. Some we'd left with Gil's parents in Zichron Ya'akov, and my Kindle had been reluctantly thrown away after it broke in my bag, a huge crack across the screen making it impossible to read. I was sad to say goodbye to my evening reading. I pulled out bits of food wrappers from various pockets where I'd lazily stashed them, moving them to our rubbish bag to be discarded at the next resupply stop. Wetting the bandana, which I often used to tie around my forehead to keep the sweat from dripping into my eyes, I began cleaning the dust from some of the gear. I dismantled my walking poles and used the last of the water to wipe away the grit from the joints where they were becoming stiff and difficult to open and close.

It didn't take me long to finish sorting through everything. Having so few possessions was a huge contrast to the way I had been living in London. I thought that living in a studio flat meant we wouldn't have a lot, but once we started pulling out items from the cupboards in preparation for leaving for the trail, it was never-ending. Clothes barely worn, kitchen items used only once, pointless souvenirs and all the latest gadgets that, at the time, we felt we so desperately needed. I wondered how much money I would have in the bank now if we hadn't bought any of that stuff. We got rid of most of what we did have, some going to charity and some being sold to fund the trek alongside the savings we were building up each month for our adventure. What was left, mostly clothes and a few sentimental pieces, was packed into a handful of boxes to be temporarily stored in my sister's loft. I didn't miss any of my things now.

Before putting everything away I counted how many items we had. There were forty-eight, with Gil's clothes, hats and sunglasses adding another sixteen, making a total of sixty-four between us. Everything we needed, each with purpose, all nicely packed on to our backs, although I would have very much welcomed the addition of a replacement Kindle to help kill a few more hours.

I settled on top of my sleeping bag, lying next to Gil who was, of course, napping, and stared up at nothing. I was bored, but OK with that fact, noting that I felt underneath something I had rarely felt before and which could only be described as contentment.

Chapter 11

Just when I thought the scenery couldn't get any more impressive, I turned a corner and Barak Gorge loomed ahead of us, a huge vertical limestone crag with a slice cut right down the middle forming the dry riverbed that we were to walk through. The light-coloured rock gives it its nickname: White Canyon. I spotted a face staring at me from one of the nooks. The beady eyes of a rock hyrax, a small creature comparable to an overweight guinea pig, were peering at me. It was only the second time I'd seen one, their shy nature and brownish-grey colouring making them hard to spot. We looked at each other for a few seconds before it turned and scuttled off back into its hiding place.

Gil and I walked in the riverbed, the walls looming either side, trying to comprehend that in a matter of months dangerous amounts of water would be flowing through here. The eroded formations made for an interesting morning as we hiked our way through the canyon, on multiple occasions clambering up and over dry waterfalls. Ladders, metal rungs and cables had been attached to the smooth surfaces to aid hikers. Reaching the top of the canyon, we kept height for six kilometres before descending, this time through Vardit Canyon. Just as had been the case with the climb up, aids had been put in place on the trickier sections. When we reached the edge of a particularly big drop, I saw metal rungs on the floor, a couple of them visible before they disappeared over the edge and out of sight. I took a few small, careful steps forward to the edge to try and get a better look, making sure not to get too close.

Chapter 11

'I'll go first,' I said, wanting to get it out of the way. Gil put out his hands to take my walking poles. On any climb that involved using our hands we would attach them to the outside of our rucksacks so they were out of the way. This got a bit tedious at times, as you needed to collapse them and then, when you wanted to use them again, reopen them to the correct height that made them comfortable for hiking.

'Just throw them down,' I said, thinking we could save some time. 'We can collect them at the bottom.'

I threw my poles over the edge and heard a clatter as they hit the ground, much further than I was anticipating. Gil leant forward and also sent his poles over the edge to join mine at the bottom. I got on my hands and knees and shuffled backwards towards the drop until I reached the first rung. Keeping my body weight as close to the wall and my hand grips as tight around the rungs as I could, I started to lower my feet one at a time. I could feel my heart pounding in my chest. *Can these rungs definitely take my weight?* I pushed the thought out of my head, knowing I had no option but to trust them.

Each time my feet knocked a rung I'd move the sole of my boot securely on to it and then shift my weight before lowering the other leg, looking for the next one. At one point, my right foot was hanging below me searching for a rung but was finding nothing but air. Although I hadn't looked down yet I could feel the presence of a big drop and space below me. Sweat was making my hands slippery so I gripped on even more tightly, my knuckles now turning white with the effort. I wanted to be off this ladder. Leaning back slightly, I braved a glance downwards, causing the adrenaline coursing through my body to intensify. The next rung was not directly below but veered sharply to the right.

'You OK?' Gil shouted down, noticing I'd stopped.

'Yep.' My voice sounded strained. I shifted my feet and adjusted my course until I was on the firm ground of a ledge. I let out a long shaky breath, wiping my hands on my shorts and, for the first time, realised my mistake. Below the drop was a basin, a dry pool, about two metres wide and two metres deep. The ladder, which I had assumed would go straight down, had actually gone down at an angle and taken me to a platform which veered around the side of the basin where our hiking sticks were now lying, very much out of reach.

We stood on the edge of the basin and looked down at our sticks on the gravel, looking teasingly close.

'I think I can get myself back out of it,' Gil said.

'Hmmm. Are you sure?'

'There's the small ledge there. It looks just about big enough that I could get a grip on my boots to push myself up and out.'

'It looks too small to me.'

'I probably shouldn't risk it.'

'I agree. It'd suck if you got stuck.'

'Unless you jump in with me and give me a push out, then I can pull you out.'

'And if the rock is too slippery for me to get a good grip, what do we do then? It's not like there's anything here you can hold to give you leverage to pull yourself out.'

'Let's see if this is long enough,' Gil said, unclipping his bracelet, a chunky band made of braided rope. Using the penknife to cut one end, we unravelled it to reveal a thin but strong piece of rope that was about three metres in length. Gil tied a sliding loop in one end then, holding on to the other end, threw it towards the sticks. It caught relatively easily on to the end of the nearest pole but, with no real features to snag on to, it was a wasted effort.

We admitted defeat, knowing we still had ten kilometres to cover before camp and had run out of ideas. We walked away leaving our poles in the basin. It felt like I was leaving behind a friend.

After eight hundred kilometres of hiking with poles, being without them felt like I was learning how to walk again. My body started hurting in new places, most notably my lower back and my thighs, and I no longer knew what to do with my arms. Gil settled on holding on to his backpack, looping his fingers into the straps, while I let mine hang awkwardly by my side.

It was dusk by the time we were putting up our tent. As we turned on the phone to get the details of our next water cache, a rare bar of signal popped up. Gil quickly started pressing buttons.

'What are you doing?'

'I'm going to post in some Israel hiking groups on Facebook. See if there's a group passing by who might be more confident about getting the sticks than us.'

'You think that's going to work?'

'Probably not. But it's worth a try.'

* * * *

The next day involved twenty-eight kilometres and eight hours of hiking on the same long road for the entire day, and all without my beloved poles to help me drive my legs forward. For the most part, the trail followed alongside the Route 40 motorway, until it collided with Shizafon junction which marked the end point of the day.

I'd read in many places that this was the most boring day on the trail and it didn't take me long to realise that was a fair description. We'd spoken with a few hikers who had planned to hitchhike or take a bus to miss it, and the guide offered a cycling option instead, providing details of a service that would drop bikes with you and meet you at the end to take them back and reunite you with your bags. Perhaps I was clinging on to my pedantic, made-up rules, but I couldn't even contemplate walking this far just to skip a stretch because it wasn't interesting. Thankfully, Gil was on board, with the same line of thinking, so we were walking it.

We decided to hike separately so we could each fall into our own pace, which naturally put me in front. I listened to podcasts, finishing off the real-life murder series we had been listening to (they definitely caught the wrong guy), and focused on the end point and our glorious day off tomorrow – our last rest day on the trail. A significant statement that it felt too soon to let fully sink in.

The only change of scenery that day came while passing a remote army base, its grounds covered with tall wire fences and CCTV cameras that followed me as I walked by. The path was littered with pellets and targets from a shooting range and in the distance I could see monstrous tanks tearing about, trailing clouds of dust and occasionally firing ammunition.

At last, and just in time as my MP3 blinked that it was about to run out of battery, Shizafon junction came into view. On the other side of the road was Neot Semadar Inn Restaurant. I went inside, a dainty bell announcing my arrival, and bathed in the cool air conditioning. Wasting no time, I made a beeline for the till where I ordered an overpriced chilled organic apple juice. I took a table by the window and gulped down my drink in two mouthfuls.

I looked up when I heard the bell again and saw Gil, a huge smile on his face.

'You won't believe it.' He passed me the phone to show me a picture. It took me a while to decipher what I was looking at. A hiking bag, not ours, with four walking poles strapped to the side.

'Those are our poles!'

'A group of young guys saw my message and were passing the canyon this morning and managed to get them. They posted this in the group saying that the sticks are in safe hands and on their way.'

'You're kidding me?'

'They're going to leave them at this restaurant,' Gil nodded at the checkout, 'and we can collect them in two days when we come back here to start walking again.'

While Gil tucked into an even more overpriced ice cream and spoke to a couple of people in the restaurant to try to hitch a lift into Neot Semadar town, which was a short drive away, I went up to the lady behind the counter. I explained about the guys who would be dropping off our walking poles and bought them some drinks and ice creams on tab as a thank you for kindly returning them to us. I hoped they would all appreciate the cold sugar as much as I had.

'I got us a lift,' Gil called to me. A man behind him in a Baja hippy jumper, with long hair sporting plaits finished with beads, gave me a wave. It was a taste of what was to come. I was about to experience a side of Israel that very few visitors get to see.

* * * *

I have always been fascinated by Israel's collective communities, known as kibbutzim. Many kibbutzim remain across Israel, although most have been privatised or lost a lot of the traditions around sharing work, money and the raising of children. One of the more communal kibbutzim still in existence, though, is Neot Semadar, our home for the next two nights.

Established in 1989, the community is built around an organic farm which is usually home to around two hundred residents. The doors to Neot Semadar are generally closed to visitors but recently, perhaps in response to their ongoing issue with dwindling numbers, they have decided to allow hikers on the Israel National Trail to stay there on the same terms as community members: food and board is covered in exchange for labour.

We'd timed our arrival perfectly for dinner. A middle-aged lady with tightly curled dark hair came to greet us, taking our hands in both of hers in a warm embrace.

'I'm Sal.' She wore a long floaty skirt and no shoes. 'Just drop your bags here. After lunch I'll show you to your room, but let's eat first. Here we wash our hands before going in.' We dutifully soaped and rinsed our hands in the sink, then followed her into a large hall. As we passed the door, she leaned towards us and in a whisper said, 'Here we don't talk while we eat.'

Inside the hall, long tables and chairs had been laid out, similar to a school dining room. Despite there being over a hundred people milling about or sat eating, there was not a word uttered. It felt sombre, like we were gathering for a wake. Grabbing a pair of seats at the table closest to us, giving apologetic looks to the people unfortunate enough to have to sit next to two hikers who hadn't showered in a week, we wasted no time tucking into the spread that lay before us. Raw vegetables of every colour, hummus and olives, plus large jugs of olive oil, all picked and made fresh on-site.

I nudged Gil, who was sitting next to me, and nodded my head trying to indicate to him to pass the salt, which was out of my reach. He shook his head with a frown. I nodded again in the direction of the salt. He looked at the table then picked up the plate of olives and passed them to me. I put my hand over my mouth to stifle a laugh.

'Salt,' I tried to mouth to him once I'd composed myself but he just shrugged. Giving up, I just stood up and leaned over him to grab it myself.

I looked around at the others on the table, taking in the many beaded bracelets and harem trousers. They seemed to be mostly young, in their twenties or early thirties, or older, in their fifties and sixties. It felt very odd not speaking and, judging by the way most people were sitting, faces down, shovelling their food as if they were in a race to get out as quickly as possible, it seemed I wasn't the only one who felt that way.

After eating, we were given a brief tour of the grounds. The dining room and the lawn outside were the centre of the community. Behind that sat a bizarre pink building with a huge phallic tower protruding out of the centre. Covered in arches and decorative windows and balconies, all painted in different shades of pinks and white, it looked like it had dropped straight out of a (questionable) Disney movie.

'That's the art centre,' Sal explained in a sing-song voice. 'You can visit that later today to find out more about our founding leader.'

We followed her to an area of residential houses which all looked identical.

'This is your house,' she said, passing us a key. We stepped inside. It was a small, plain studio apartment. A double bed sat in the middle. There was a writing desk and chair, a little kitchenette and a separate bathroom. 'I'll leave you to settle in. We meet at 5am in the morning in the centre for work duties. Oh, and tonight we are doing a stretching session on the lawn at 7pm if you'd like to join.'

'Five-bloody-am,' I said, when Sal had gone and we'd closed the door. That was a painful wake-up for a rest day.

'At least maybe we'll get the work part done with early and can then just enjoy the rest of the day.'

We both settled into our new temporary home and I set about the task of trying to wash the straps of my bag in the sink, scrubbing them together with hand soap into a froth before rinsing them through. The straps sat in my armpits as I walked and, at the end of a long day, the stench was like something that didn't belong on this earth. I didn't even know it was possible to feel sick from your own body odour, but after a few sweaty days the straps would get so bad I had to breathe through my mouth. No matter how many times I washed and rinsed them, the smell never entirely went away.

Once the straps were as clean as I could get them, and I'd handwashed my clothes and showered, I debated whether to go to the stretching session Sal had told us about. I concluded that my muscles, which were getting stiffer and sorer by the day, could probably do with a bit of attention. It had been ages since I'd done any yoga and, even if I wasn't feeling like it now, I knew I always felt better after a session. Gil, who was chatting to his mum on the phone, decided to stay behind.

It was now dark and, with a lack of street lighting outside, I could barely see anything. I was running five minutes late so I hurried as fast as I could in the direction of the centre while also making sure I stepped carefully in my sandals. The last thing I needed was a stubbed toe to add to my discomfort. Nearing the lawn I heard a strange sound. Through the bushes I could make out the large hall where we'd eaten earlier and in front of it, lit up by stadium lights, the lawn. I shuffled forward, keeping myself hidden by in the dark bushes so no-one would see me.

'Meow, meow.' There were about twenty people, all moving about in different directions, their arms wildly flailing, their heads lolling, and everyone was meowing like cats. I watched for a few more seconds trying to take in the situation before quietly retreating and making my way back to the studio.

'What happened to the yoga?' Gil asked, after telling his mum to hold on a second.

'Everyone was just pretending to be a cat.'

'What?'

'Just don't ask.'

* * * *

The early wake-up on a rest day was just as painful as I had anticipated. Opening the front door, we saw dark figures coming from all directions, lethargically making their way to the centre as if being drawn by a magnet. One of the dark figures shushed our conversation as we stepped out to join them. We hadn't realised we weren't meant to be talking now either.

The large hall had been cleared of tables and chairs. We were handed hot lemongrass tea and all sat in a circle on the floor. I struggled to keep my eyes open as the following twenty minutes of silence dragged on until a man started playing some mediocre music on a guitar. This seemed to be the cue that it was time to work. The kibbutz had lots going on to make income, from a restaurant, vegetable garden and winery, to art workshops, goat farm and olive plantation. Other community duties included the day-to-day running of the kitchen and schools, and maintenance. Gil was posted in olive production and I was sent to the goat farm.

A middle-aged man, who had a distinct smell and look of goat, introduced himself as Noam, keeper of the goats. I tried to make small talk but could see he was a man of few words – except when he randomly turned to me at one point and declared, 'There's a nice feeling here,' as I followed him to the farm. *Did he mean between us?* I didn't know what to say so I opted for saying nothing at all, which seemed to be favoured by the residents here anyway.

Noam showed me how to set up the machines to milk the goats, who were all waiting patiently at the door when we arrived at their paddock. I didn't enjoy seeing animals cooped up or farmed but was interested to learn more about what was involved, as it was something I'd never seen before. While I was sweeping the floors Noam came up to me.

'Do you drive?'

'Yes.'

'Good. These are the keys to the tractor.'

'Oh. Um, I can drive a car, but I've never driven a tractor before.'

'That doesn't matter. It's easy. You push the lever forward to go forward. Push it back to go back.' He handed me a pair of keys. 'Take the tractor in the yard with the hay on the back to the field opposite. Put the hay out to feed the goats.' And with that he walked off.

I clambered up and sat on top of the tractor, the seat bouncing up and down as it took my weight. It took me a long time to even work out how to turn the thing on but, once I had, I tested the lever, clicking it into first gear to go forward, and was pleased that the tractor started setting off at a very slow pace. Once past the gate, I began to turn the large, upward-facing wheel until I heard a crunching of metal behind me. Quickly slamming on the brakes, I looked around and saw that the attached trailer, which was carrying the hay, had caught the corner of the gate. I hadn't given myself a wide enough berth. Swearing under my breath I reversed a bit, shuffled forward but stopped again, realising the trailer was about to collide for a second time. It took three more attempts before I finally got enough of a wide berth to get the tractor and the trailer out of the yard. Only then did I notice Noam in a neighbouring field leaning on a rake watching me.

I reached the field and parked the tractor next to a large metal grate which I assumed was the feeding station. Grabbing a fork from the back I began to move the hay from the trailer into the grate, covering myself with dustings with each scoop. I was working hard, enjoying the physical challenge of using my arms instead of my legs for a change. Just as I was about to scoop the last of the hay, Noam strolled into the field and I waited for my praise as I was sure I'd done the task in record time.

'You are meant to split it.'

'Huh?'

He waved a hand further down the field where I noticed a number of other smaller grates dotted about.

'You are meant to split it,' he repeated, more slowly.

I blinked at him a few times.

'The hay. You are meant to split it. How can the goats feed properly if it's all in one place?'

I didn't have a response to his question because I'd never seen goats feed before, let alone taken responsibility for dishing out their meals. I picked up the fork and began the demoralising task of returning the hay back to the trailer so I could transport it to the other grates.

Noam stayed longer than I would have liked, studying me in silence with his striking grey eyes, all the while chewing on a piece of hay that hung from his mouth.

'I bet you don't get many city folk working here?' I said to him, trying to lighten the mood. He gave a half-nod, then left me to it.

I was wiped by the time I returned the tractor to the yard, and covered head to toe in hay. There was some satisfaction in physical labour and getting so much done before 9.30am, but I was now starving, longing for a rest and very ready to catch up with Gil. The goat workers were all gathered inside on mismatched plastic chairs around Noam so I joined them. We did some more sitting in silence. I shifted noisily in my chair trying to disguise the sound of my persistent stomach rumbles.

'I have something I want to share,' Noam finally said, breaking the silence. 'Internally, I feel I was very quick to judge someone. I should learn to be more patient and accept others' inabilities.'

My cheeks started to burn.

A few more quiet moments passed before Noam announced, 'Let's have breakfast.' I jumped up and practically ran back to the dining hall. Gil was already there and I joined his table and began filling my plate. It was so frustrating not being able to ask him how his morning had been or to share with him how the Goat Man had made me the focus of his morning reflections. Still, the priority was to eat. Just as I was finishing up my third plateful of food, an announcement was made for everyone to meet on the lawn. Another circle, a much-loved shape in Neot Semadar it would seem, was formed outside and the community elders listed the tasks for the day, asking for volunteers for various things, as well as sharing news like, 'We are keeping a flame alight for thirty days if anyone would like to help and take a four-hour shift.' The meeting ended and just as I was about to turn to Gil to start sharing my strange morning, Sal came up to us.

'We now go for our second work shift of the day. I thought it would be nice for you to try something different, so Gil, you will be helping in the kitchen, and Bex, you will be working in the olive factory.'

Reluctantly, I followed Sal to the factory, stifling a yawn along the way. 'So how many shifts do you work in a day?'

'Three shifts of four hours,' Sal replied. I groaned internally, imagining another eight hours of work ahead of me.

'And how many days do you work?'

'Everyone works six days a week. Shabbat is a rest day.' I did the sums in my head. Seventy-two hours of work a week for basic food and board.

At the factory I was kitted out with a hairnet and apron and was set up in front of a huge barrel of olives. My task was to take a large glass jar and fill it with olives, leaving about two centimetres of space at the top.

It didn't come as a surprise when I was told, 'We like to work in silence.'

The first hour of filling jars passed quickly, but then the task started to become tedious. I found myself trying to work faster and faster in the hope that I would eventually empty the barrel, or the jars would run out, but any time I got close it was promptly refilled. My head was starting to spin staring into the barrel of olives. My eyesight was playing tricks, making everything look like it was swimming.

We did have a couple of short breaks, but they were more exhausting than the factory work. We sat together and had meaningful discussions.

'Let's discuss ways that we had limits put on us as children. Bex, would you like to start?'

'Ummmmm. I think I'd like to just listen this morning.'

When we reached four hours and all headed back to the centre I was exhausted. It would have been a lot easier if we could have just chatted a bit once in a while to help the time pass.

After another silent feeding, Sal approached us again for our next work duty.

'Sal, I'm really sorry,' I said, cutting her off before she could speak, 'we have an important work call soon that we can't miss. I didn't realise we'd be working at this time otherwise I would have rescheduled it.'

'That's OK,' Sal said kindly and without question, making me feel even worse for lying, 'you can just skip the next work shift. You can stay an extra day if you like and experience more tomorrow?'

'Thanks. We'll have a think,' I replied with a smile.

It was such a relief to finally be able to sit down for a minute and speak with my husband, and about nothing meaningful or deep. For the rest of the afternoon we hid out in our studio room, afraid that if we were to leave we might get drawn back into doing more work. I didn't feel totally bad for skipping out on our duties as we still had some hikers' chores to do. Plus, I needed to catch up on my blog. It had been the most tiring rest day yet, and had also felt like the longest. Usually rest days flew by in a flash, but Neot Semadar had rewarded us with drawn-out time if nothing else.

Unsurprisingly, we decided not to take Sal up on her offer of another day and we let her know before heading in for our final meal that night. Dinner was a lot more enjoyable after having had a break and I even didn't mind having a bit of silence to eat yet another wonderful organic vegetarian meal. I avoided the bowl of olives, though.

Chapter 12

Neot Semadar had been an interesting experience but I was ready to make my escape. The next morning we decided to join the pre-dawn meditation just so that we could cheekily help ourselves to the freshly baked bread and homemade jam that followed. I snuck a couple of extra pieces of bread into my pocket when no-one was looking. We'd planned to stock up for the last time in Neot Semadar Inn Restaurant, our only resupply option in the area. We needed enough food to take us to the end of the trail, now less than a week away. While waiting for our lift to the kibbutz we'd browsed the shelves, but there had been very few suitable options available, other than some dates and cereal bars, all of which were, of course, overpriced. We added them to the two pasta meals and handful of snacks that we had leftover from the last stretch. It would be enough to keep us moving but not enough to keep us from being notably hungry.

I wasn't worried, though, safe in the knowledge that there had been one sure thing on the trail – we were a target for feeding. Most people who passed us made sure we were left with food in our hands. It was a type of generosity that I'd never experienced anywhere before and, as a hiker permanently thinking about food, it was the kindest and most indulgent thing anyone could do for us. On more than one occasion we'd even ended up with too much food. Not wanting to turn down others' generosity we would find ourselves overflowing with snacks so would then be on the lookout for another hiker to offload them on to. Even though we were unlikely to pass many people between now and Eilat, I was sure at least one meal would be taken care of in this way.

One of the workers, who was heading back to the restaurant to start a shift, gave us a lift in his pick-up truck. Bouncing around on the bumpy track, I sat in the back of the truck on top of some sacks watching the art centre's pink and white phallic tower move away from us. *What a strange place to choose to live*, I thought to myself. All the rules and reflections weren't for me. That said, I appreciated that places like this existed, places where people were just doing their own thing, different to what the rest of the world might call normal.

Jumping out of the truck, I headed straight to the restaurant, where I spotted our walking poles leant up against the wall behind the till. It was strangely emotional having them back, my hands finding their place through the loops and on to the familiar grips with ease. I hadn't realised it was possible to become so fond of a pair of inanimate metal poles.

Before leaving, I asked the lady behind the till if the boys had been given the food and drinks we'd left them. She nodded and told me they had been happy. The simple act of kindness from these boys, who we would likely never meet, would make all the difference to the hours of walking we still had ahead.

Sticking to our usual rule of not hanging about in the mornings and putting off the inevitable difficult first hour, we threw on our bags, waved our final thanks to the staff and headed out towards the rising sun. We walked over an empty tarmac road stretching far off into the distance, before cutting into the surrounding landscape. We were leaving behind a lot of the larger mountain ranges and craters here, facing instead flat spaces interrupted by small, rocky mountains.

I could feel my body was stiff in new places, mostly my arms and shoulders, from yesterday's work in the goat farm and filling olive jars.

At one point, the gravel underfoot turned to fine sand, becoming deeper and deeper until it morphed into a huge mound. We'd reached the Kasui Sand Dunes and a handful of perfectly formed, sweeping dunes now sat in our way. It was as if someone had deposited a huge load of sand in the otherwise rocky land that surrounded us. We had been magically transported to the Sahara Desert.

'This is what I thought the desert would look like,' I said to Gil as we began the momentous effort of climbing up the edge of the first dune. My feet and poles disappeared into the sand with each step and I had to tap into all my leg muscles to crawl my way out of the sunken holes. After reaching the end of the knife-edge and pausing at the top to take a photo, I started down the other side, slowly at first but then speeding up, going with my body weight and the sand moving underneath me as I ran down the dune. Gil was catching up with me so I sped up to race him to the bottom, although he was past me and back on to gravel before I was even halfway down. I instantly regretted my decision to run down, as my shoes started filling with sand. We both sat on our bags and emptied our boots, using our socks to try and rid as much of it from between our toes as possible.

Shortly after, we reached another local phenomenon, a prehistoric archaeological site called Uvda Leopard Temple. Ahead was a rectangular space marked out by a single metal bar, no higher than my knee. At one end of the barrier was a sign, so faded and torn I couldn't make out most of what it said, except for the instruction to keep a metre away.

On the floor were drawings made from rocks embedded in the ground. These are believed to be four thousand to six thousand years old and are just randomly here in the desert, open and unprotected.

They supposedly portray leopards, although they didn't look like leopards to me. They looked like square shapes with stick legs, the sort of drawing a toddler might make that could represent anything with legs, from your mum to a pet dog. I perched on the end of the barrier and resisted the urge to touch them.

Being physically worn out from our rest day meant I was longing for a lunch break earlier than usual so, even though we'd only been going for four hours, I told Gil I was hungry and ready for a break. I rummaged in my bag and distributed the small amount of rations we had to last us for the rest of the day. A piece of bread, some raisins and a snack bar each. My stomach rumbled slightly but I didn't pay it much attention. With the end in sight, the next few days had a different quality to them and suddenly it didn't matter so much if I was hungry, tired or sore, because it all felt incredibly temporary. Since leaving Neot Semadar we were on one big countdown to the end. It created an urgency to my thought process as the amount of time we had to ponder, to plan, to daydream, suddenly didn't feel so infinite. There was a pressing need to conclude and decide.

'Less than a week, Bex,' Gil said in between mouthfuls of raisins, his thinking clearly in harmony with mine.

'I know, I keep thinking the same. I just can't get my head around the fact this is nearly all over.'

I looked down at my brown Hanwag hiking boots. They had started the hike shiny and smooth but were now battered, lined with creases and a shade of faded colour similar to the desert around me. I'd been reluctant to buy them when I'd found out they would set me back £200, but now that didn't seem such a big price to pay for a pair of boots that had carried me safely for such a long distance.

'How do you feel about finishing?' I asked.

'Excited, I think. But it also feels a bit strange. I've spent a lot of the trek thinking about finishing but now it's almost over I'm not so sure I do want it to end. I'm tired and I want to stop hiking, I definitely need a proper break to rest and stay still. But it's kind of been cool being in the desert, you know. Just doing lots of walking, not having to think about work, plus we've been able to spend so much time together. It's been good.'

'Yeah, it has been good. What are you going to do first when we finish?'

'Shower. Then eat a massive pizza. Or maybe I'll eat first then shower. Or do them both at the same time.'

'I was hoping you'd say shave.'

Gil ran his fingers through his scratchy beard. 'I was thinking of keeping it.' It was the longest he had ever gone without shaving. His facial hair was patchy and spiky and made my skin red every time he kissed me.

'I'm definitely filing for a divorce, then.' I popped the last of the bread into my mouth, wishing it had something on it for flavour. 'A pizza does sound good, though. And honey on toast.'

'Still daydreaming about honey, then?'

'You have no idea.'

Hours after having this conversation we stopped again for another break, after having just been rewarded with a view of the Arava valley, as well as the Edom mountains which sat in Jordan, across the nearby border. Near where we sat, strange potato-shaped rocks were scattered on the side of the cliff. The Red Book explained that they were limestone nodules, calcite sedimentary rocks that had crystallised around organic species, proof that a sea had covered the area fifty million years ago. As I read this aloud to Gil, two men, one older and one younger, appeared in the distance, meandering their way up the path we were about to follow down. It was very unusual to see day hikers midweek and when they reached us the older man explained that he was out hiking with his son before he started his army service.

'We wanted to finish the entire trail before he started,' the father explained. 'We've been doing it one day at a time over many years. We needed to get some extra days in if we are to finish it in time.'

'How do you get back to the start each day?' Gil asked.

'Both my wife and I drive two cars to the end point of the day. I leave my car there for when we finish hiking. My wife then drops us at the starting point and goes home. We've enjoyed doing this together very much.' He glanced sideways at his son.

'How many days do you have left to do?'

'Nine after this one.'

'That's amazing,' I said, thinking of all the hiking we'd done and all the logistics that must have been involved in doing it in segments. As well as how much driving up and down the country his wife had been doing to make this a possibility for them. The dad said something in Hebrew to his son who then took off his pack and began rummaging through the bag. He produced a packet of crisps and rolls and, digging deeper into the bag, pulled out a squidgy tub of honey. My mouth dropped open a bit.

'Here, take these.'

'Are you sure? Do you have enough?' I said, already feeling my mouth salivating at the sight of the golden honey.

'Of course, of course. Tonight we have a home-cooked meal. You need this more than us. You've still got a lot of tough hiking before you reach Eilat.'

'*Toda raba*,' thank you, Gil and I said in unison, taking the food from the boy's outstretched hands.

'We are actually running low on food supplies, so this is really great,' Gil said.

'Especially the honey,' I added. 'I was literally just saying how much I've been craving it. I've been thinking about it for days!'

The father smiled at me in a way that made me think he didn't quite believe me. After checking that we were OK for water as well, they wished us luck for the rest of our hike and went on their way.

Gil looked at me and held up the honey in his hand. 'The trail really does provide,' he said, shaking his head in disbelief.

'It bloody well does.' I grabbed the honey and squeezed a small amount straight into my mouth. I couldn't wait to finish off the rest later, in the soft rolls, for dinner.

That saying, 'The Trail Provides', was one I'd come across a few times while researching our trip. Used by hikers, and believed to have originated from the popular Pacific Crest Trail in the United States, it refers to moments of magic and serendipity that occur while on a long-distance journey. On more than one occasion we'd been longing for or in need of something and, somehow, it would manifest. Like craving honey for days and passing a rare hiker who just happens to gift you some. Or losing your hiking sticks down a hole and then for a group to coincidently see a post about it who also just happen to be passing the exact area so they can fetch them and bring them back to you a day later. Or, my favourite example:

'We've run out of toilet paper,' I informed Gil in a deadpan voice as we set off one morning having just done my morning wee. I might normally have saved the last piece for a more urgent time but I had thought we had another stash.

'You sure there aren't any spare bits in your bag?'

'I've checked. Twice. There's nothing.' After water and food, being stuck in the desert without toilet paper, days from the nearest shop, is up there in terms of bad situations. The desert offers nothing as a substitute. No streams or soft moss, just a lot of rubble, sand and spiky shrubbery.

Later that day, after pondering all our very bleak options, we were meandering through a wadi and Gil was some way ahead when I heard him yell out. At first I thought it was the flies, as they'd been particularly persistent that day. As I neared, though, I saw what had caused the excitement. Gil was frozen, eyes huge in disbelief, holding up a box of soft pink three-ply tissues. The top tissue was poking out in a perfect triangle from the opening, as if it had been purposefully positioned for us.

'It was just sat there, right in the middle of the path!'

We had given each other a celebratory hug as if England had just won the Rugby World Cup.

It was another coincidence that allowed me the comfortable illusion that there was a greater force than us on the trail. Reassuring me that no matter the problem, everything would find a way of sorting itself out, even if I couldn't always see how.

* * * *

When the alarm went off, my first thought was that maybe I would stay in bed, call work and fake an illness, until I opened my eyes and I realised where I was. There was no boss waiting for me today. We barely set alarms anymore, our bodies accustomed to getting up before sunrise without the need of a shrill awakening, but today we had an ambitious plan and to make it happen we needed to set off as early as possible.

We hadn't met many long-distance hikers on the trail, far fewer than I had expected having read stories of the popular American and European trails which sometimes see thousands, from all over the world, attempting to hike their full stretch each year. This had been a lonely trail, and not one that seemed to be attempted by many foreigners. Among the few hikers we had met, a number had dropped out, returning home or moving on to new ventures. Stories of their departures would become gossip on the trail, reaching us if we were ever to pass another hiker. This was how we heard the news of Eitan, the seventeen-year-old we'd met while staying in the warehouse before climbing Mount Tabor. Gil's prediction had come true. Just hours after we'd left him he had fallen badly, breaking his leg in the process. It was the end of his time on the trail and, possibly, I wondered, of him starting his army service. I just hoped he had managed to get help quickly.

Ayal and Gadi – and Yoni and Dan, who we'd briefly met near the start of the desert stretch – were our only trail friends who had made it this far. Although we'd met them all separately, they'd ended up hiking the trail together in one group and were just a day ahead of us. Gil had been messaging with Ayal and had made a plan to meet with them so we could spend our penultimate day on the trail together. It was an opportunity to celebrate the last night in company. It also meant a 34-kilometre day to reach them in time, with some pretty significant climbs along the way.

'You think we can make it?' Gil asked as we expertly rolled the tent to the perfect dimensions to fit in its storage bag.

'Physically, yes. It'll just be a race getting it done before dark.'

Knowing we had nine hundred and fifty kilometres behind us, and having enjoyed a rare restful night's sleep, I set out for the day in high spirits. We were not far from Timna National Park, an area rich in copper ore, which has been mined since the fifth millennium BCE. Green and blue patches litter the area and the valley is also home to towering sandstone columns known as Solomon's Pillars.

We were less than an hour from the entrance of the national park when we passed a group of a dozen chatty teenagers out on a day trip, bubbling with the excitement of being on their own and away from school. We'd been expecting them, as just ten minutes before we had passed two of their supervisors who were leaving bits of paper under rocks. They explained they were leaving clues that the students had to solve as part of a navigation challenge.

I stepped aside on the rocky narrow path to make space for the group to pass us, returning their exaggerated 'hellos' as they went. Too distracted, watching the funny dynamics of a group of teens dressed like adults, but acting like small children, I didn't pay much attention when I stepped back on to the path. Because of this, my foot caught on a protruding rock. Instinctively, my other foot lurched forward to try to stop myself from falling over, but it came in contact with my walking pole. I had been walking with the pole strap looped around my hand and so, when my foot collided, it stopped dead with nowhere to go. I was now flying head first towards the rocky ground below me, my arms and legs all tied up with no way of cushioning the impact.

In that split second before I hit the rock, I braced myself for the pain. My head hit the ground first. Gravity pushed my heavy rucksack up my shoulders, causing a sharp pain to shoot through my neck and down my arms. A wave of nausea rolled over me. I was wedged awkwardly, head down in the rocks, my bag pinning me down. I tried to move my arms out so I could lift myself up but they were both stuck, caught in the walking pole loops. I couldn't move.

Gil was with me in a second. He unclipped the straps and eased the bag off my back, removed my poles and then slowly helped me turn over until I was in a seated position. I blinked, hearing the blood rushing in my ears, and saw the group of teenagers all frozen, staring wide-eyed at me.

'Tell them to go,' I whispered to Gil. I could already feel the prickle of hot tears reaching my eyes. Gil exchanged a few words with them and they moved on, a couple of them looking genuinely worried, turning back to check on me as they left.

My shaking hand went instinctively to my head and when I pulled it back there was blood.

'Are you OK?' Gil asked, taking a look at my head.

'Yeah.' It was mostly my neck that hurt.

'Just keep really still for now, don't move your neck yet.' While Gil examined the cut on my head I assessed the rest of my body. There was a large graze on one knee. I wriggled my arms and legs and they seemed fine, nothing more than scratched and bruised.

'Your head's OK. There's a cut, but not big enough for stitches.' He pulled out a bandage from our first-aid kit and, pushing it to my head, told me to hold it while he checked the graze on my leg. Feeling a bit less dizzy, I tried moving my neck, slowly turning it left and right, then up and down. I was relieved that moving it didn't cause any more pain. It was stiff and I couldn't turn it all the way, but it was nowhere near as bad as I initially thought.

'Is anywhere else hurting?' Gil asked.

'No. My neck is a bit sore but it's OK. I really thought I'd damaged myself badly. It hurt so much when I hit the ground.'

'Just take it easy for a bit. You can move all your arms and legs OK?'

'They're fine.'

'You really scared me.' He put his hand on his chest. 'That was a big fall.'

He leant in to give me a hug and I buried my head in his shoulder, unable to stop the tears from coming, tender from the vulnerability of falling. In those few seconds I lay pinned to the floor, I was sure my moment of stupidity had ended the hike.

Using most of our remaining water, knowing we weren't far from the national park entrance where there would be a receptionist and water supply, Gil cleaned the cuts and grazes before applying antiseptic cream. My hands eventually stopped shaking.

'How are you feeling now?'

'Just really tired,' I said, taking a deep breath then curling up and leaning against my backpack. My mind was about to tell me to give up on our plans for today, to give up on hiking so I could lie in our tent instead, until I remembered a time when I was seven. I broke my arm falling off my bike – for some reason there was a brick in the middle of the path and, when I rounded the corner, I swerved to try and miss it and came straight off. Despite having a fracture in my left arm, it was the gruesome graze on the side of my body that I cried about when I hobbled home to my mum. For this reason, the fracture went unnoticed for another week, the swelling put down to nothing more than a sprain. That was until I forgot about my sore arm, lost in conversation with my mum after she'd picked me up from Brownies one night, and unthinkingly yanked the car door shut. I screamed out. The pain in that moment was far more intense than anything I had felt when I'd initially fallen off my bike, and my mum took me straight to hospital. For six more weeks I had to wear a cast until, at last, it was removed. The first thing I did when I got home from the hospital was run around the back of the house to open the garage so I could go out on my bike. It didn't even occur to me that I should be afraid of riding it anymore.

I thought of that little girl now as I sat by the side of the path, curled up, wishing more than anything I could just be in the comfort of my old home, tucked under a thick duvet, watching films and eating plum jam sandwiches. For a week, aged seven, I had walked around with a broken arm protected by nothing but a cheap arm wrap my mum had picked up at the pharmacy. I'd played netball in PE, awkwardly trying to catch a ball with one hand, showed off to my godfather how I could do handbrake turns on my pedal go-kart, and did nothing more than wince when my teacher had grabbed my arm to put it on my piece of paper, telling me that, even though it was sore, I still needed to hold the paper to make sure my handwriting was steady. There was a badass, fearless girl somewhere inside me, even if I didn't always know it.

I took Gil's hand and pulled myself on to my feet, taking a few tentative steps, and then tried with my rucksack on. I had an ache flaring at the back of my head and my grazes and bruises stung, especially on my left elbow where there was a particularly angry bruise forming, but I was fine. I could move. I wiped away the tears and took the lead, ignoring the feeling that each rock was out to trip me. Pushing down the fear, I concentrated on my successes and not my failures. I'd taken a few stumbles, this one the worst, but I'd also taken a million steps without falling. That had to count for something.

* * * *

We were losing light fast but I needed a rest. I sat down and Gil hovered nearby, both of us looking off towards the Jordanian mountain range looming in the distance. The setting sun was casting dark red scars on the mountains, making them look like they were on fire. I yawned again, struggling to keep my heavy eyelids open.

'We're nearly there, just another hour or so and all on flat. You've done great.' Gil came over and planted a kiss on my head.

'They don't even look real.' I nodded towards the mountains. 'I have a real urge to go there.'

'What, right now? You want to hike the Jordan Trail? We can start on Monday.'

'Maybe I'll take a week off first to catch up with sleep. But in all seriousness, I do want to visit one day; just look how beautiful they are.'

Gil looked at the sunset. 'Bex, I know you're tired but we really do need to get moving. It's just a little bit further and then you can rest. I'll make dinner tonight, you don't have to do anything.'

With a big sigh, I lifted my stiff body up from the rock.

We continued after both throwing on jumpers, the temperature dropping dramatically as it did each evening. As the light around us turned from orange to grey we put on our head torches. It was a cloudy night, so once the last of the sunlight had gone the space around us turned to a claustrophobic blanket of black. My mind was too tired to think so I just let it zone out as I walked behind Gil, matching his pace, my light shining on his legs, calf muscles I'd never seen before bulging with each step.

A loud wolf whistle broke me from my trance. We both stopped and looked up. In the distance I could make out torches waving at us in the darkness and the slight flicker of a campfire, its sight warming me even from this far.

We reached the boys in camp and all slapped hands in greeting, unanimous in the decision that hugging when we were all this smelly and dirty was something none of us wanted. They crowded around us as we set up camp, sharing various stories from the day and asking to see my injuries when I told them I'd taken a fall. There was a lot of admiration and questions about our gear.

'Your tent is like a spaceship,' Yoni said about our MSR Hubba Hubba two-man tent. Israeli outdoor gear was mostly military, dated and simple, the sort you'd expect to see old Boy Scouts using while out on a camping trip.

Gil kept his promise to make dinner that night, the last main meal we had in our bag: pasta with a stock cube. I finished it quickly then sat around the fire as I listened to the conversations about our time on the trail. We hadn't spent a huge amount of time with these men and I knew very little about them. I couldn't tell you their surnames, how they would usually spend their weekends or what sort of clothes they wore when not hiking. Still, I felt a closeness and unity with them. Like we all shared a secret, were part of an exclusive club that others didn't understand and that by default gave us a unique sense of belonging and togetherness. Although I also felt something else. A nagging jealousy, not wanting to share the trail and its experience, which felt like it belonged personally to me and me alone, regardless of all the feet that had taken the same path before me.

It had been a long and testing day and I needed my sleeping bag, so I left the group and retreated to the tent. Once inside, I took one last look at the bruises and grazes on my body and then fished out the beanie from my bag. I pulled it over my head, liking the cosy way it felt against my cut. Laying down, I looked up at the netting above me. This little contraption had become my second home. Tomorrow we would put it up and sleep in it for the last night on the trail. Where home would be after that I didn't know, but there was comfort in thinking this tent would always be close to hand should I need it.

Chapter 13

It didn't matter that I'd climbed a hundred mountains and hills to reach this point, it still took an incredible amount of willpower to get up any incline that stood in my way. I'd wrongly assumed that there would be a point on the trail where I would be suddenly super-fit but, being so close to the end, it was clear the six-pack, toned version of myself, bounding up mountains like a gazelle, was not going to make an appearance any time soon. There was an undeniable sturdiness and endurance to my fitness now, but still, any climb came with sweat, bright red cheeks and a lot of effort.

This crag was particularly steep, with large, jagged rocks that I grabbed to steady myself as I climbed. I paused briefly on a natural platform and looked up, amazed to see that the boys had already made it to the top. Running up climbs was something they all did, racing each other to see who would be first.

'It's better to get the climbs over and done with quickly,' Dan had said to me earlier that morning when I had asked them why they were running.

It was only when hiking with others that it became so apparent just how many rituals and routines we all had. There were many ways to hike a hike. Making decisions around food, taking breaks, choosing camps, calculating distances, packing bags and setting paces: everyone had their own way of doing things.

Gil and I had resigned ourselves to letting go of all our rituals and slot into the group. However, running uphill was not something I was about to take on. I just didn't have the physical strength to move that fast with my pack. Gil seemed to be relishing the challenge (or the competition), though, leaving me tailing behind. I was feeling very slow and the pressure of having to keep up with the group made the climb even harder than it was.

By the time I reached the top, Dan and Yoni had already boiled water to make Arabic coffee, which they were pouring into mugs. Ayal was passing round a bag of seeds. I settled myself into a comfy space knowing we'd be here for a while. This was another difference. We kept our breaks short, while the boys liked to take long and regular breaks and each time, without fail, the stove would be lit and coffee passed round, regardless of the fact that we were all sitting in thirty-degrees heat.

'Have you seen it?' Gil asked.

I gave him a puzzled look and he lifted his coffee cup, indicating I should look south.

Shimmering on the horizon, only just visible against the blue sky, was the Red Sea. I could make out Eilat, the resort destination popular with Israelis. On the other side of the bay was Jordan and the town of Aqaba, a huge Jordanian flag flying high – so big I could recognise it from where we were. A grin stretched across my face. We were so close, the end was just there, within touching distance. It looked like it was nothing more than a few hours' walk from where I stood, although I knew we still had a day and a half of hiking before we'd get there.

We sat in silence for a while, except for the soft click of Gadi's camera as he moved about snapping photos of the view but, mostly, of us. It still amazed me that he had carried the clunky camera all this way.

The coffee kit was packed away back in its pouch and this seemed to be the indicator that we were leaving. I pushed myself up using the ground to steady myself and let out a groan as my knees and hips straightened out after a long time sitting still. We'd been hiking for nearly two months now and my body was really starting to feel it; a deep-rooted weariness had stiffened my joints along with a tiredness that no amount of sleep seemed to ease.

We fell into a line as we meandered down the other side of the crag. Heading towards sea level meant the rest of the walk was mostly downhill. It was a day of canyons and cliffs, of towering pillars and magnificent formations and I savoured it all knowing it was slipping away from me, the same way you slow down to enjoy chocolate as you near the end of the box. On flat sections the group would congregate together in a pack to chat and make jokes.

'I'm going to hang back and listen to my music,' I said to no-one in particular on one of these stretches. I slowed my pace and they broke off ahead of me. I was enjoying the company but had my limits. Much of the day's conversation kept steering back to a WhatsApp group they were in called *Farts Only*. They all found it comical, and I found it comical that they found it so comical, even after hours of listening to recordings that seemed to be sent from all over Israel. I was happy to see Gil chatting in Hebrew and laughing with friends but seeing them ahead cemented a feeling that had been growing over the last few weeks. I was missing female company. It had been such a long time since I'd spoken with a woman, something I noticed even more in the outdoors, where bravado and arrogance seemed prevalent. It was a space where I found myself acting differently when in a group of men and, even more poignantly, where I was often treated differently.

It was not the first time in my life that I became acutely aware of my gender. The first was as a child, when I was what most people would describe as a tomboy. At the tender age of six, one of my first school reports said, '*Rebecca needs to learn it's OK to be a girl.*' I was actually OK with being a girl. I was just less OK with all the restrictions that seemed to come with being a girl, all the rules about what to say, how to act and what to wear, because for a lot of the time I just preferred the 'boy' options. It was not surprising that as the teachers struggled to accept me this way so did the students, and being different from gendered stereotypes made me a target for teasing in the earlier years and, worse, exclusion in the later years.

In preparation for doing the Israel hike I had decided it was sensible to sign up to courses that would teach me the skills I would need to get me across a desert safely. To learn how to read a map, how to choose a wild camping spot and how to administer first aid should anything happen. It was on these courses, my first exposure to the world of outdoors adventure, that, for the second time, my gender kept me from fitting in. The courses were intended to boost my confidence, but I often found I left them with increased insecurity and more certainty that I didn't belong. There was so much competitiveness and one-upmanship, so much snobbery, celebrations reserved only for those who could go the furthest or fastest. My unfit and inexperienced self could never compete.

One of the worst experiences I had was on a course where, as usual, I was the only woman. It was the final day, and I was being assessed on my ability to lead a team and to navigate, along with other basic outdoor skills. We were taking it in turns to lead the group as a way of demonstrating our skills and, when it was my go, I had a particularly tricky section to pass, which involved stepping over a gap. As I'd been shown in training, I positioned myself securely so I was blocking the open space that posed the biggest risk of falling, where I could act as a physical barrier but also provide reassurance if a group member might be nervous. I instructed the team to step across one at a time. The first man came forward and, completely ignoring my instructions, decided to take an entirely different route to the one I had just asked him to follow, muttering 'This way's easier' as he went. The next man followed him.

'They clearly have an issue taking instructions from a woman,' the assessor told me after this behaviour continued for a while, by which point my mind was permanently questioning every decision I was making. 'You need to be more assertive.'

Being more assertive didn't work, though. The digs continued, from the 'Come on lads!' that was shouted out after breaks to the time the instructor told me that I don't need to eat as much as I think I do – this after I had asked him twice if we could stop for lunch as it was pushing mid-afternoon. I sat eating my sandwich, feeling every bulge on my body, wishing I had the guts to tell him, 'Well, you try walking all day on your period without eating.'

I was surprised that I passed the course because, surely, anyone who received the level of criticism I had could not be good enough?

'You don't seem very excited,' Gil said to me in the car as he drove me home. It had been one of the toughest and most miserable experiences of my life, despite the fact I had passed and that it should have been one of my biggest achievements. I was downtrodden and confused by it all. These men weren't mean – we got on fine in the pub in the evenings – but the second we all put on our rucksacks something changed.

Gender inequality in the outdoors didn't just manifest itself in the adventure groups and courses I was joining. I noticed it in sponsorship and media coverage, reserved mostly for white privileged men, and while looking for gear for my hike. One day, I visited a popular outdoor shop in central London in search of a hat and after asking the shop assistant where I could find them, he took me to the range for women. It largely consisted of straw hats with colourful ribbons around them and a few caps, mostly pink and purple.

'Are these suitable for a hike in the desert?' I asked.

The shop assistant glanced at the range then let out one booming laugh. 'No, none of them are. You want something with UV protection and a rim.'

'Do you sell hats like that?'

'We do. They're in the men's section.' He led me to a different level in the shop and pointed to the men's range, which was full of technical materials and useful features from hidden pockets and drawstring neck cords.

'You know, I've never noticed that before,' he said to me as I paid. 'It's pretty insulting.'

I was glad he agreed.

* * * *

I turned off my music and pulled out my earphones when I saw Gil hanging back from the group so he could speak to me.

'What are you thinking about?' he asked.

'About setting up that group I was talking about.'

An idea had been forming and spilling out as I came closer to the end of the hike. What had started as an idea for an online magazine to help inspire and connect more women to get outdoors had morphed into the notion of a community. A space where women could go on adventures, without competition or judgement, where teamwork and support could help build confidence.

'Bex, I think it's the best idea you've ever had. Except maybe hiking this trail. I was thinking, though, you should launch it with something exciting, like an adventure, just to show what it's all about.'

'I was thinking exactly the same. I've actually already got an idea for an adventure. It would need to be local and cheap but also still a bit of a challenge. I thought maybe a team of women might try and climb the height of Everest in the Lake District over five days.'

'I like it. You could call it the Everest Adventure.'

'You really think women will apply, though? I mean, they don't even know who I am and it's not like I've got loads of experience.'

'You've just hiked one thousand kilometres! How much more experience do you need?'

'Yeah, but, you know what I mean.'

'Not really.'

'I'm being serious. I'm worried no-one would apply.'

'Is it something you'd apply to join?'

'In a heartbeat. In fact, I love the idea of being selected for a team adventure and doing something with a group of women. It sounds fun.'

'Then I guarantee other women will feel the same way too.' I knew that Gil would unconditionally praise any idea I had with absolute support and enthusiasm, it was one of the reasons I loved him so much and felt so blessed to have him as a partner, but still, his words reassured me.

'OK.'

'OK?'

'Yeah, OK. I'm doing it. Decided.' Gil held out his hand and I slapped it as if sealing the deal.

For the rest of the day I let the excitement of future plans, adventures and doing something that I never thought I'd be brave enough to do sink in.

* * * *

I puffed up the sleeping bag to act as a cushion and then leaned back on my rucksack. It was the closest I could get to a comfy seat on the trail, using only the possessions I carried with me. I was half in the tent for shade, my legs dangling out of the open door and porch. It was the last camp of the trail, a large, flat space shadowed by a mountain on one side and with a road on the other. It wasn't the nicest campsite by far after weeks of being spoilt with natural spots without a road or quarry in sight, but at least the road wasn't busy and I only had to look towards the mountain to be reminded of the nature we would be leaving behind.

The boys were making the most of the wide space and were playing frisbee, moving back after each throw to see how wide they could make the gap. They'd invited me to join in but I had declined. I wanted to relax and use the last couple of hours we had to write my daily blog while I eagerly awaited the arrival of food. A couple of the boys' mums were travelling to the campsite to meet us, promising to bring home-cooked goodies with them.

It felt like a significant blog post knowing I would have only one more left to conclude the journey. Despite my attempts at writing and rewriting, I couldn't quite articulate how I was feeling as all my thoughts seemed to be swirling in an internal mess as I switched from one emotion to the next. Once I finished, I looked through some of the messages and comments I'd received. Kind words from loved ones and strangers alike, all wishing us well as we completed the trail. Each comment made me feel a little better about my writing, a bit more sure that my blog was worth continuing with. I had so much gratitude to them all for following my journey, for taking the time to read my misspelt ramblings before leaving me a message.

By the time I finished thanking everyone individually, the temperature had dropped drastically and a strong breeze had picked up. I reached into my bag and pulled on my fleece, one of my most loved items. It provided a pillow at night to rest my head and a warm embrace when I needed it. My stomach rumbled. Gil and I had no food left, having finished the last of our nuts at lunchtime that day.

When the convoy of mums arrived, all the boys rushed to the cars like a hungry pack of wolves. I couldn't remember whose mum was whose, and the way they greeted everyone individually, enveloping us all with maternal hugs, made it impossible to tell. The boots were opened and bags filled with containers carried over to the campsite where there was a fire already lit.

'This is Jachnun,' Ayal said, passing me a box which I'd been eyeing up as it made its way around the group. 'It's a traditional Jewish dish. You slow-cook it overnight.'

Inside lay a long sliver of pastry accompanied by a thick tomato salsa. I eagerly scooped some into my camping pot before taking a bite. My taste buds tingled, overloaded with flavour. It was slightly sweet and dense, and tasted like it was made of pure calories, just what my ravenous stomach wanted. More food was passed around: a warming vegetable soup, a creamy Arabic dessert called muhallebi and a fresh loaf from which we all tore large chunks.

A bottle of whiskey was passed along. It had been our contribution for the evening. We'd given Ayal some money and instructed him to ask his mum to collect something we could all drink to celebrate.

'What shall I tell her to get?' Ayal had asked.

'Whiskey,' I'd said instantly, thinking it the only drink suitable to mark the ending of an adventure. Everyone took a big swig from the bottle, before grimacing. They clearly enjoyed whiskey as much as I did. When it was my turn I lifted the bottle high, embracing the burn of the liquid as it made its way down my throat. I took another big swig before passing it on.

'Urgh,' I said, shaking my head. I'd barely drunk anything for two months so it didn't take long for the alcohol to take effect, warming my insides and fogging my head with a fuzzy glow.

The wind was really starting to pick up now, not that any of the others in the group seemed to notice. English had switched to Hebrew and the stories were becoming more exaggerated, fuelled by the drink. I'd brought my sleeping bag to sit on but now pulled it out from under me to wrap tightly around my body, leaning back into a low wall that circled the fire area to shelter myself from the wind.

Gil passed me the bottle again but I shook my head. 'I'm good, thanks. I'm just taking it all in.' Dan and Yoni were now on their feet and seemed to be re-enacting a dramatic tale.

I looked up just as the clouds parted, creating a window to the stars. I watched the lights glistening brightly and hoped that there would be many more nights like this where I was outside, by a fire, enjoying the biggest wild we have, the space above our heads. The warmth in my chest seemed to extend beyond just the effects of the alcohol. Perhaps this was the glow of knowing that tomorrow I was going to complete the biggest challenge I'd ever set out to achieve.

Chapter 13

Or maybe it was the sureness I felt that everything was going to be better from now on. Either way, life was good and I was ready to step back into the world beyond the trail. I just needed one more day to close the chapter.

Chapter 14

It had been fun spending time with the boys, but this day was not meant to be shared. It was too personal, too big, too significant. Gil and I had started the trail together, exactly fifty-two days earlier, on a dusty track near the border of Syria and Lebanon, and today we would be finishing it together, reaching the shores of the Red Sea.

Everything today was a last. The last time I slipped my feet into my heavy boots, doing up the shoelaces that were now stiff and coarse. The last time I deflated our sleeping mats, then helped Gil dismantle the tent. The last time I stuffed my sleeping bag into the bottom of my pack before expertly placing each of the items I carried, knowing exactly where everything went so it all fitted with ease. The last time I did a double-check of the campsite, sweeping the floor to make sure we hadn't forgotten anything. The last time I hoisted my backpack on, doing up the straps, adjusting my walking poles, making sure everything was just so before setting off, taking the first steps on the last day on the Israel National Trail.

The nearby road was empty of cars and the boys were all still sleeping in their tents, silent except for some gentle snoring and the occasional rustle of a sleeping bag. I found the early morning silence peaceful rather than empty. I walked past the tents, careful with my footing so as not to wake them. We didn't need to say goodbye as we had already arranged to meet that night for dinner in a restaurant in Eilat. It was hard to contemplate that by then we would all be sitting clean around a dining table, our time on the trail would be done and we would be easing ourselves back into the world we had left behind.

I fell into my usual hiking rhythm, the patter of my feet and the thud of my hiking sticks tapping the ground like a drum. I hadn't slept a great deal the night before. I could have blamed the wind, which had picked up in the early hours and whipped around our tent, causing it to shake and bend at an alarming rate, but that wasn't the real reason. There was too much anticipation about the day ahead, making it difficult to find restful sleep. I kept thinking of the bed we would be sleeping in that night. We had booked to stay in The Shelter, a hostel run by a religious couple celebrating 'Jews for Jesus'. I knew that a stay there would come with religious reading material and a bit of pressure to join their daily gatherings, but their generosity was too good to turn down. The owners, who had walked the entirety of the INT, offered two free nights to any hiker who finished the trail. We had considered splashing out, staying in a fancy hotel to celebrate our huge undertaking. Before our departure we had saved a few thousand to cover the cost of the hike but it had come in considerably cheaper than we had expected – with travel, insurance, food and accommodation all coming in at the equivalent of just $700 each – so there was money to burn if we wanted. Instead, we opted to celebrate by learning how to dive, putting the rest away carefully so we didn't have to rush back to our jobs. Plus, like Neot Semadar, staying at The Shelter felt like something of a necessity, something you couldn't skip if you wanted the full INT experience. I imagined myself checking in and folding away my walking poles into my rucksack, hoping not to see them until my aching body had healed and all the trail's struggles had faded to nothing but nostalgia and fond, distorted memories.

I was excited to finish the day, but first I had to cover fourteen kilometres of hiking. Our climb down to sea level continued, with over six hundred metres of descent. Half an hour in, though, we had to tackle Mount Shlomo and the strenuous climb to the top, where we were rewarded with more panoramic views of the sea ahead, which was gradually creeping closer.

The hike seemed to be going painfully slowly and I had to stop myself asking Gil what the time was every fifteen minutes. Instead, I hung back, letting him take the lead. I noticed he walked taller today, shoulders back, and his head whipped about, taking in everything around him, unable to settle on anything in particular. My wonderful hiking companion who I had sometimes argued with over petty annoyances on the trail and who needed reminding regularly to not be so serious, but who had spoilt me with support and companionship along the way.

Making our way down the other side of Mount Shlomo, I was especially careful with my footing, as on some parts the loose rocks underfoot slipped away from me. I'd read that most accidents on mountains happen when hikers are coming down, when they lose concentration after putting all their energies into going up. As I battled with my mind, which was constantly pulling my focus towards the end point, I could understand why.

At first we saw just a spattering of day hikers but, the nearer we got to the coast, the groups of people increased in size. Day hiking is a popular activity for tourists in Eilat, eager to see some of the desert which sits immediately behind the cliffs on the coast, although most of them only venture a short distance. Many of the hikers returned my over-eager smiles, often looking curiously at our cumbersome rucksacks – or maybe they were just taking in our generally grubby state. I had to resist the urge to tell everyone we passed that we had walked all the way from the other side of the country.

'Excuse me.' A couple, both with short, very blond hair, waved to us. 'Do you know where we are on this map?' the man asked with a Scandinavian accent, holding out a map that was printed on the back of a leaflet.

We both walked up to him, not getting too close as we were always very conscious of our hikers' stench. Looking at the map I spotted the INT path and saw the contour lines of the canyon we had just meandered through before coming out into a slight clearing.

'We're here,' I said confidently, pointing to a crag in the clearing which we were standing next to. My heart dropped. I'd made such an effort to not look at a map or check the time that I hadn't realised we were so close to finishing. We were just a couple of kilometres from the large area of blue which represented the sea. The end was really coming.

'Do you think life will be different after this?' Gil had asked a few nights back while I sat cross-legged outside the tent, him lying inside, waiting for our couscous to finish cooking.

I gave the contents of the pot a stir. 'I know it will be. I don't think life will ever be the same for us. This has been such an amazing experience. Really life-changing, you know? Or maybe life-affirming is a better phrase. I just know I can't go back to what we had before, not if I want to be happy.'

'I've been thinking the same. I decided I want to do something different for work from now on.'

'Like what?'

'I don't know yet. I just know that I want to try working for myself and to build something up rather than just working for others. I don't ever want to deal with office politics again, I can see now how much it used to affect me. And I'd be pretty happy if I never had to wear a tie again. I feel like I'm not the same person anymore.'

'You're not. You've definitely changed.'

'In what way?'

'Calmer, more relaxed, more confident. Just more yourself, I guess.'

'Like I was when we first met travelling?' I'd often talk about the youthful and fun Gil-From-The-Early-Days who had faded away at some point along the way.

'No. You're not like that Gil anymore, either. You can't stay young forever. You do seem happier in yourself, though, and less distracted.'

Gil chewed the corner of his lip and after a moment's thought said, 'You've changed too, you know?'

'Oh, I know.' I could feel it inside. The turmoil of negative thoughts, the constant chatter in my head and the tightness that sat on my chest had all lifted. It was a release of something I'd been holding on to with both hands clenched, something that had been fogging my vision and weighing me down in all that I did. Sometimes, on the tougher sections on the trail, I would imagine that I was literally pounding out all the negativity and insecurities from my body, driving them out and leaving them behind me on the path. Memories of hurt, confusion and betrayal soaked into the ground along with the dripping sweat I left behind. There was no need to carry them with me any longer; the weight of my bag was heavy enough as it was.

We left the Scandinavians after checking they had enough water with them – we weren't able to pass on the generosity of snacks or food, as we were down to nothing but crumbs – and fell into a silent walk. In no time at all we found ourselves standing next to each other looking up at a hill. It wasn't a big hill. There were no major switchbacks, just a path that led straight up to the top.

'This is it, Bex. The last climb. On the other side is Eilat.'

'Let's do it, then.'

'You don't want to wait a little bit first?'

'Wait for what?'

'I don't know,' Gil laughed, 'it just feels like we should do something significant. It's really strange that this is finally it.'

'It is. It definitely feels like there should be something more. Maybe a fanfare or a big crowd to cheer us to the end.'

'That would be nice. It feels a bit anticlimactic.'

'I kind of like it this way.'

We paused a moment longer while I tried to think of something we could do that might mark the occasion. Nothing came to mind.

'Can we go now?' I said.

'Yeah.'

We both started towards the bottom of the hill, this time me in front. There were a few people about, although I wasn't paying much attention to them. The only thing that mattered now was me, Gil and this hill. We'd barely made it more than a few steps, though, when a man wearing a navy NY cap, which he had on back to front, came up to us.

'Where are you hiking from?' I recognised his British accent immediately. Behind him, bent over slightly and dripping with sweat was, I assumed, his girlfriend.

'We've actually walked all the way from the north of Israel,' I replied. It crossed my mind to make up a less exciting story as I was so eager to tackle this damn hill already, but I couldn't help myself.

'What? Like, as in one go?'

'Yep. There's a trail that goes the full length of the country, over a thousand kilometres.'

'That's amazing.'

'Thanks. This is actually our last climb of the whole trek. We're about to finish it.'

'That's amazing,' he repeated.

'You out on a day hike?'

'Yes, just from Eilat. I wish I was doing something like you, though. Wouldn't that be cool, Rachel?' Rachel didn't answer but just frowned slightly and then looked at me with a strained smile.

'You should do it – it's been tough but also an incredible journey. Well, enjoy the rest of your day. We're keen to get to the end and into a shower. It's been a while!' I gave a stiff half-wave and started on the track that led us upwards.

'So how do you shower and get water?' the guy said, jogging slightly to catch up with me rather than staying behind as I had hoped.

'Oh, um, we use something called water caching. Someone drops water for you at a designated place each night. And you just don't shower. Or you do but only when you pass a hostel or somewhere you can stay for the night and get clean.'

'How long has it taken you to do the whole thing?'

'About eight weeks.'

'Where do you sleep each night?'

'In a tent. We've got everything we need in our bags.'

'Shall we take a break?' Gil asked, coming up alongside me.

We both stepped to the side and took a seat on the floor and I pulled out the map to indicate we were stopping for a while. The guy came and sat next to us and Rachel let out an audible sigh.

'Take a seat,' the NY man said to Rachel.

'I'm having a great time standing, thanks,' she said more than a little sarcastically, making me squirm a bit with the awkwardness. This guy really wasn't getting the hint from any persons present. This was a moment I'd been daydreaming about since day one. A moment I'd played over in my head, wondering how I'd feel and if it'd be as epic as I imagined. We'd barely seen any people for a month and somehow, just at the most significant point of the trail, an annoying Brit, only the second one I'd met in Israel, had decided to latch on to us.

'What about snakes? Aren't there dangerous snakes?'

'We've only seen a few and they don't bother us. Where are you heading?'

'Nowhere in particular. That way I guess.' He pointed in the direction we were going, although I was sure they'd been heading the other way when we'd passed them. Gil and I exchanged a look and I knew he was thinking the same as me. There was only one way to lose this leech: power up this hill with everything we had. Gil and I jumped up before he could ask another question. We hadn't bothered taking our backpacks off so all we needed to do was grab hold of our poles and start pushing on.

'We'd better be off. Lovely to meet you both!' I said, already making my way up the hill, Gil close at my heels. After a few paces I half-glanced back and saw that they were still following us. I picked up the pace even more. I was close to running. It didn't matter how much energy this took because ahead of me I had infinite rest days. After a few minutes, sweat began to drip from my nose but I didn't slow down.

'*Why are we running?*' I heard Rachel hiss from behind. Glancing back I saw the guy look behind him to a death stare from his girlfriend. She wasn't taking another step. He looked up at us in disappointment as we sped further ahead and then back to his girlfriend before, finally, admitting defeat.

Despite the fact we'd lost them we didn't slow down. The further we climbed, the more I relished the energy that was coursing through my body. All the hiking we'd done was pushing me upwards like a physical force.

Less than one hundred metres to the top.

I thought of all the thousands of metres we'd climbed to get here. All the sleepless nights, the tantrums, frustrations and tears. Of all those times I thought about quitting, sure I would never make it. Of just how tough it had been pushing my body and my mind like never before.

Seventy metres to go.

I thought of all the times, nestled in the difficulties, that were full of laughter, smiles and moments of sheer joy. Of the pure resilience and determination I'd mustered from depths I didn't know I had.

Fifty metres to go.

I thought of all the people who had supported us in so many different ways, from my loving husband, to family, to the wonderfully kind Israelis, strangers we'd passed along the way who had hosted and fed us. And of how much that generosity had meant. How much it had filled me with reassurance and a need to continue to pass on that goodness to others.

Thirty metres to go.

I thought of all that precious time I had spent in nature. All the beauty. Exploring a land rich and diverse and oozing with history, passing mountains, seas and desert crawling with hidden ecosystems and creatures who would sometimes grace us with their presence.

Twenty metres to go.

I thought of how I'd set out on this trail to prove something to myself and others. To feel worthy. And how it no longer mattered 'why'. It only mattered, completed or not, that I had actually given it a go. In my own way, at my own pace, I'd done it. There was nothing to prove, only experiences and learning to be gained.

Ten metres to go.

The path flattened out and the top was in sight. This was it.

Two metres to go.

I took the last few steps and looked at the sea that reached out in front of us just a stone's throw away. Yes, this moment was as epic as I'd imagined. I was overwhelmed with emotion. We hugged, both with tears in our eyes, neither of us saying anything. We didn't need words; that crystal-clear blue water marked, so perfectly, the accomplishment of the hot, dry desert trail we were saying goodbye to.

We ran down the hill and at the end of the path reached a scruffy car park and a small makeshift sign that said we'd reached the end of the Israel National Trail. It was the most underwhelming of endings but in a way seemed absolutely appropriate. Rough around the edges with no frills attached, yet to the point and efficient: this was Israel.

This wasn't the real ending, though; there was still one more thing to do. We crossed the road on to a beach dotted with tourists burning in the sun and children building sandcastles. Running down to the water's edge, we dropped the rucksacks and walking poles on the sand before pulling off our boots and socks. We grabbed each other's hands and ran, fully clothed, into the water. I took a deep breath and submerged myself, staying under for as long as my lungs could stand, feeling like the pores in my cracked, hot skin were soaking up the water and cooling off from months of exposure.

The trail had felt like it would never end but now, just like that, it was over: slowly, and then all at once. I wanted this moment and this feeling to last forever, but eventually I had to come up for air. I wiped the water from my face, seeing a crowd of baffled faces all sitting up on their sunloungers or pausing from their books to stare at the strange couple who'd just gatecrashed their luxury holiday to run fully clothed into the sea. We both burst out laughing and let out a whoop.

'Food?' Gil asked, after a few more minutes floating on the water.

I was already up and making my way to the falafel stand.

Epilogue

I never noticed that the trail has a distinct smell until I returned to it some years later – two, to be precise. It smells like a disused attic, mixed with the smell you get from drying earth after rain on a sunny day. I paused and inhaled deeply, filling my lungs to capacity. The smell was comforting and safe and instantly brought back all the memories I had carved in these rocks.

The Negev was just how I left it. Striking, hot and still. Only this time a little bit less quiet as I had the company of five other women who provided plenty of chat and banter to pass the hiking hours. They were all now perched in a line on the edge of Ma'ale Yemin, a dry waterfall overlooking a deep canyon two hundred metres below, about half a day's hike from Makhtesh Katan, the 'Small Crater'. We'd just been enjoying the six-second echo that comes with the view, taking it in turns to shout and howl into the open space, listening to our voices as they bounced around the mountains and then off into the distance.

Excitement had radiated from the team all morning, embracing how alive it makes you feel to be walking somewhere so old and yet that somehow feels so new and undiscovered. We were all here as individuals who had never met before this week, but were united as a rare group of foreigners hiking where few tourists go. It was an energy that could only be found on an adventure, and our friendships had been forged as quick as lightning, heightened in this kind and encouraging team sharing this unique experience together.

I grabbed a snack bar from the side of my bag and went to take a seat next to my team. I had sat in the same spot with Gil two years ago while we watched a field mouse scavenge our lunch crumbs. The lady who had sat with him then was very different to the one that sat here now. I'd accomplished so much in that time. I had focused my attention and taken steps, a few every day, towards the dreams that I wanted to manifest in my life. Recognised that I had been born with a huge amount of privilege and had so much to be grateful for – not endless wealth, but things that mattered even more like health, an education and loved ones. It was time to start appreciating my good fortunes by seeking out the opportunities that were there and working hard to change the things that were very much within my control, while accepting the things that weren't.

I launched Love Her Wild, growing a community, taking hundreds, and then thousands, of women on adventures all over the world. I gave talks to huge audiences, reached over a million people with my writing and got recognised with multiple awards. I discovered I had a natural entrepreneurial spirit, and realised career successes that I'd never thought I would be capable of achieving – and, maybe, didn't even know were an option, having always believed there was only one linear route available when it came to building a livelihood. I could see clearly how my schooling had failed to give me what mattered most, not qualifications and grades, but self-belief and an understanding that available opportunities are for me as much as anyone else. I built a career throwing myself into projects I liked, using my skills to my advantage, chasing the things that worked and moving on swiftly from the things that didn't, and pursuing a passion that, underneath it all, was driven by a genuine desire to make a positive difference. The pride from seeing how women benefitted from Love Her Wild was like nothing I'd felt before. I saw how adventures boosted women's well-being and helped them realise just how much they were capable of. The changes they experienced seeped into their lives, leading them in new directions and often towards the simple but life-altering act of carving out more time to do the things they loved. I'd created an incredible community which outgrew me and became testament to all the brave and kind women who make it what it is today.

Alongside finding a career that mattered to me, I had created a life on my terms, taking the parts of the trail with me that made most sense. I'd stepped away from consumerism and the chase for promotion, and had no intentions of going back. My life became busier in one sense, running a business and travelling more than ever before, but much slower in another. Taking time to be in nature always took priority, as did looking after my mind and body with meditation, yoga and walks. Realising those small daily habits and connections were what mattered most.

It had seemed like such a big, scary thing dismantling our lives to do the INT, but I could see now that the thing I had feared most, being left with nothing, had provided me with my biggest advantage. The trail had given me a blank canvas, everything stripped back inside and out, the tight knots of our ties loosened. Finishing the hike was like stepping out into the world as an adult for the first time again, where a hundred branches of possibilities lay before me – only this time it was better, because now I was more confident, more sure of what I wanted and more resilient in the face of pressures and setbacks. Going on an adventure had truly been the greatest gift I'd ever given myself.

After a rollercoaster few days in the Negev desert with my team of Love Her Wild women, mostly due to unprecedented flash floods that meant I had to continually adapt our hiking plans, we found ourselves in Jerusalem. Saying the last goodbye to them the next morning, I had an overwhelming urge to mark the occasion and knew exactly how.

Heading into the Old City of Jerusalem, I turned down a hidden side street off the main tourist path where I found Razzouk Tattoos, one of the oldest tattoo businesses in the world, dating back twenty-seven generations of the same family. Today the shop was run by Wassim who, when I entered, was hunched over his desk drawing. His shoulder-length black hair covered most of his face but not enough that I didn't immediately notice his striking dark eyes.

Too quickly, I found myself lying face down at the back of the tiny shop, staring at the exposed brickwork while Wassim began the process of stabbing me repeatedly with a small needle. He was a man who picked his words carefully and, although he didn't smile much, there was a warmth about him.

'You must get a lot of different people passing through the shop,' I said, trying to distract myself from the building sharp pain.

'Yes.'

'Are they mostly Christian pilgrims?' I asked, knowing that historically these were the people his family would tattoo as they passed the gates of the Old City.

'No. Keep still.'

'Sorry,' I said, now biting down on a scarf, trying to urge my body to stay still while he repeatedly scratched back and forth over the same raw area of skin. There was a long pause while he focused on tattooing and I focused on not moving, using the mantra I had repeated many times on the trail: *this will pass.*

Some time later, Wassim paused to fiddle with something on his device. He clicked the machine back on and turned to continue tattooing, but stopped and looked at me. 'I tattoo people of all religions and none, I don't care what religion anyone is. It doesn't matter who or what you believe in, only that you are living true to yourself. That's how life is meant to be lived, I believe.' He turned his attention back to the tattoo.

The strange significance of Wassim's words played in my head that afternoon as I walked cobbled streets, getting lost in the winding maze of the Old City, visiting each of Jerusalem's four quarters: Muslim, Jewish, Christian and Armenian. Absorbing the mayhem that each turn brought, I picked up irresistible treats from the markets along the way.

Occasionally, my hand would reach behind to tentatively touch the bandage where my shiny new tattoo sat, the skin still red and tender. Now inked there permanently was the black outline of a *hamsa*, an amulet shaped like the palm of a hand, with a tree of life silhouetted within it. Together they were a personal symbol, a reminder of the journey that had changed my life.

Wassim had got it right. Time in nature, where I could just be, had taught me a great lesson. It led me to realise there was another way, an easier, lighter way. A shortcut to having a happier and fuller life. I didn't have to stay in work that made me unhappy just so it didn't look bad on a piece of paper titled 'CV'. I didn't have to be a perfect English student to be a writer. I didn't have to chase money, possessions, careers and a routine that wasn't working for me, just because everyone else was doing so. I didn't have to look a certain way because it was expected of me. I didn't have to hide my opinions or tone down my need to take charge because others couldn't accept it. I didn't have to listen to the criticisms, pressures and expectations that sounded in my ear endlessly from others but also from my internal critic.

I only had to be myself. I only had to live true to myself. I only had to know that I am enough, exactly the way I am.

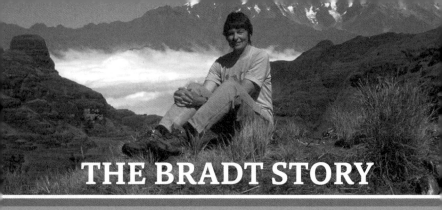

THE BRADT STORY

In the beginning
It all began in 1974 on an Amazon river barge. During an 18-month trip through South America, two adventurous young backpackers – Hilary Bradt and her then husband, George – decided to write about the hiking trails they had discovered through the Andes. *Backpacking Along Ancient Ways in Peru and Bolivia* included the very first descriptions of the Inca Trail. It was the start of a colourful journey to becoming one of the best-loved travel publishers in the world; you can read the full story on our website (www.bradtguides.com/ourstory).

Getting there first
Hilary quickly gained a reputation for being a true travel pioneer, and in the 1980s she started to focus on guides to places overlooked by other publishers. The Bradt Guides list became a roll call of guidebook 'firsts'. We published the first guide to Madagascar, followed by Mauritius, Czechoslovakia and Vietnam. The 1990s saw the beginning of our extensive coverage of Africa: Tanzania, Uganda, South Africa, and Eritrea. Later, post-conflict guides became a feature: Rwanda, Mozambique, Angola, Sierra Leone, Bosnia and Kosovo.

Comprehensive – and with a conscience
Today, we are the world's largest independently owned travel publisher, with more than 200 titles, from full-country and wildlife guides to Slow Travel guides like this one. However, our ethos remains unchanged. Hilary is still keenly involved, and we still get there first: two-thirds of Bradt guides have no direct competition.

But we don't just get there first. Our guides are also known for being more comprehensive than any other series. We avoid templates and tick-lists. Each guide is a one-of-a-kind expression of an expert author's interests, knowledge and enthusiasm for telling it how it really is.

And a commitment to wildlife, conservation and respect for local communities has always been at the heart of our books. Bradt Guides was championing sustainable travel before any other guidebook publisher.

Thank you!
We can only do what we do because of the support of readers like you – people who value less-obvious experiences, less-visited places and a more thoughtful approach to travel. Those who, like us, take travel seriously.

Bradt GUIDES
TRAVEL TAKEN SERIOUSLY